Our Georgia

Our Georgia

The devastating murder of my daughter by a killer
who should have been stopped

LYNNETTE WILLIAMS
with ROBIN EVELEIGH

Published in 2023 by Mardle Books
15 Church Road
London, SW13 9HE
www.mardlebooks.com

Text © 2023 Lynnette Williams

Paperback ISBN 9781914451607
eBook ISBN 9781914451737

A CIP catalogue record for this book is available from the British
Library.

Every reasonable effort has been made to trace copyright-holders
of material reproduced in this book, but if any have been
inadvertently overlooked the publishers would be glad to hear
from them.

Printed in the UK
10 9 8 7 6 5 4 3 2 1

MIX
Paper | Supporting
responsible forestry
FSC® C171272

In memory of Georgia Lynnette Williams, a beautiful human being, loving, caring, full of life, who would help anyone in need. She deserved a long, happy life, but was let down by the careless.

1995–2013
See you later.

Some names have been changed to protect people's identities.

PREFACE

I gasped as Georgia's smiling face filled the TV screen. It was the photo I'd given to the police earlier that day. Her auburn hair, the vivid blue of her end-of-school prom dress, seemed to glow in TV high definition.

Calling the police had felt like admitting we knew something was wrong, admitting we knew Georgia wasn't really sleeping over at one of her mate's, or off on an impromptu camping trip with her boyfriend. Now we sat huddled anxiously together in the front room. There was no warning that Georgia's disappearance would be on the evening news. Of course, we were grateful for the publicity – but we weren't prepared for it. We weren't ready for what it meant, and where we were heading.

We stayed up into the small hours before I climbed, shattered, into bed. Steve, meanwhile, stood guard in his pyjamas and dressing gown at the window, peering into the darkness outside. Despite my exhaustion, sleep was impossible. I couldn't get that picture of Georgia on our TV out of my head. It was yet another development that was turning our worst nightmare into horrifying reality.

It was half past five in the morning when our restless peace was broken by a firm knock on the front door. I threw off the covers and dashed downstairs to find Steve in the hall, heading to open it. Two figures were visible through the frosted glass. They looked bulky, neither of them Georgia-shaped. In fact, they looked decidedly police officer-shaped, I realised.

Steve opened the door to two colleagues from work: Detective Superintendent Adrian McGee and Chief Inspector Steven Tonks. The way they shuffled uneasily, shoulders slumped, uncomfortable in their own skins, spoke volumes. They knew that whatever they said, however they said it, our lives were about to be torn apart.

ONE

It was summer, 1990. I clinked glasses with my workmate, Linda, as we wound down after another busy week over a curry at a favourite spot in Bridgnorth. Linda was calm and level-headed in work, but outside of it we always had such a laugh together – meals out, picnics and trips to the coast.

"Cheers!" I said, before hooking a thumb into the waistband of my skirt and realising, not for the first time, how snug it felt. *Maybe I didn't need that onion bhaji after all,* I pondered. *Eyes bigger than your tummy!* When I thought about it, half my wardrobe barely fit me these days. Mornings meant battling with unwilling zips and awkward buttonholes. But there was no point fretting over my waistline now, not with a plate of chicken tikka masala to demolish.

"Are you boring Steve to death with more police stories?" Linda asked her husband, Gordon, sat beside her.

"Doubt it!" I said. "He can't get enough of them!"

Between mouthfuls of biryani, my husband Steve was grilling Gordon about his job as a uniformed beat bobby based at Malinsgate police station. Whenever the four of us got together, he always had a few tales to tell about his time patrolling the mean streets of Telford. As usual, Steve's eyes lit up as he drank in the news of Gordon's latest escapades. I could see the cogs whirring in his head, ideas and long-held ambitions tumbling into place.

Steve had had his sights set on the police right from school, only his height had gone against him. Back then it didn't matter if you had the sleuthing skills of Sherlock Holmes – you had to measure up in feet and inches or they turned you down flat. By the time he got to sixth form, Steve was still only 5"3", a whopping five inches short of the minimum height requirement. So when the police held a cadet recruiting day at the college, the visiting sergeant brutally clipped his wings there and then.

"Sorry, you're too short," he shrugged.

Just to drive his point home, instead of talking Steve through the application process, or geeing him up with a little bit of encouragement, the sergeant pulled out a growth chart. "From experience, you'll always be too short," he said, kicking Steve's dreams to the gutter. "Look at the chart – there's no way you're going to grow another five inches."

No – there would be no chasing burglars and breaking up scraps in pubs for Steve. Instead, it seemed his future lay in the quiet hum of the office at a metal fabrication company, Bayliss, Jones & Bayliss, over in Wolverhampton. They specialised in top-end steel fencing and gates – the stuff you see circling the Royal Parks in London, or Westminster estates – and they made a lot of money replacing the ornamental iron work that had been torn down to make weapons in the First and Second World Wars.

When we'd been kids, on the cusp of leaving our school days behind and still uncertain how we were going to make our way in the world, the careers advisors they sent you to were a total waste of time. Instead of nurturing ambition, they expected you to just knuckle under and take whatever was on offer. We both came from working class families – Steve's dad Dennis worked in foundries, and his mum Madge was a cleaner. My own mum, Jean, also cleaned, and did a stint on the shop floor in Woolworths, while my dad John drove a JCB. No one ever encouraged us to aim for a future any different to our parents'. So – given our backgrounds – a job in an office was seen as a giant step up. For Steve's family, working behind a desk, wearing a suit and tie every day, was a big deal. Walking around Wolverhampton with his grandad, the old man would glow with pride as he introduced Steve to his friends: "This is my grandson. He works in an office!" It was the first thing out of his mouth, because it was such a huge thing then.

After being pushed into the job, Steve had quickly worked his way up the ladder to the position of draughtsman estimator. The work was tame, routine, in comparison to the police, but there was no denying the money was good. Only just lately – after ten years of marriage – Steve had started dragging his feet over breakfast. While I busied around him, looking forward to another day with the girls at Boots, Steve seemed to be bearing the weight of the world on his shoulders.

"What's up, love?" I'd ask.

He'd reply with a sigh: "I really don't want to go in."

The problem was, with each promotion, the job got more and more monotonous. A decent wage alone wasn't enough. And although Steve never missed a day, he just wasn't satisfied, because he knew exactly what he was going into each morning. He gave the job the same diligence and meticulous attention to detail as the day he'd started as a teenager, but by now he could do it standing on his head. They say money doesn't bring you happiness, and it certainly didn't for Steve at that time.

What else could he do, though?

Well – thanks to Gordon – he had a good idea where he wanted to apply his skills next. By now, the police weren't so bothered about height and, in any case, Steve had proved the recruitment sergeant and his daft charts wrong. He'd grown to a willowy 6'1" – more than tall enough to hold his own hauling drunks into the back of a police van.

"What if I tried out for the Specials?" Steve suggested a couple of weeks later. We'd been to a few social dos with Gordon and Linda, and already felt at home among the other police couples. Steve just needed to see if the job really was for him. Working as a Special Constable was a part-time, voluntary role. They supported the regular police on patrols and other duties, and sometimes worked as standalone officers if it was called for. I thought a weekend post would be just the ticket.

"You'll regret it forever if you don't at least give it a try," I told him.

Every other weekend, Steve began putting in a couple of night shifts with our local force, West Mercia Police. Sure enough, from day one, he was bursting with new-found energy, returning home in the early hours of the morning with a totally different look and feel about him, and itching to tell me all about what he'd seen and done. Some nights he'd be stationed outside Cascades disco, breaking up fights when everyone spilled out at closing time, other times he'd be tearing down the street after some crook, police boots booming on the paving stones. Compared to weekday evenings when he returned from the office worn down with boredom, it was a complete turnaround.

While Steve was wrestling with a career-changing decision and weighing up leaving his job behind for a fresh start, I absolutely loved mine. I'd been working for Boots since my college days, bouncing around between departments as I worked my way up. Usually, the local branch recruited its Saturday staff from the posh girls' school. It was a point of pride for me that I was the first they'd taken on from the local comp. At 24 I was named regional assistant of the year, and by the time Steve was considering joining the police, I was working as a roving Boots sales representative based in Mumbles on the South Wales coast, visiting hospitals, doctors' surgeries and nursing homes.

One Monday morning I was getting ready for another week on the road in Wales. Pulling on my suit trousers, I took a deep breath and sucked in my tummy before doing up the top button. *These really are getting ridiculously tight!* I thought.

Steve gave me a sideways look, one eyebrow cocked, and said: "I'm wondering if you should maybe go and see a doctor."

"Really? You don't think…"

Steve shrugged, as if to say, *you never know.*

"No! I don't think so," I said, then kissed him goodbye. "I'd better get going. I'll call you."

As the week went by, alongside the swelling in my belly, I felt a nervous anticipation. Steve and I had thought about having kids a couple of years earlier but it just hadn't happened. Not that we were in any rush. In the ten years we'd been married, we carried on as though we were still courting – clubbing at the weekends, up to Birmingham or Nottingham, and holidays to Ibiza. We loved going to concerts, and Steve had a handle on all the backstreet haunts where new, up-and-coming bands played. We liked eating out and dressing well. Career-focused and earning decent wages, we enjoyed comfortable living with no money worries. Every time one of us got promoted at work, we used the bump in our income to move another rung up the property ladder, so we'd been moving house every couple of years. And I felt we'd earned our little comforts. Things hadn't always been so easy. We were strict about living within our means, and never bought on credit. Our first home had been a run-down little miners' cottage, where we'd cosy up on a hand-me-down sofa. The TV was an old black and white, hooked up to a disc recorder liberated from a skip at Steve's work.

Friday came, and I set off on the long drive along the M4 and up the M5 back to Shropshire. I'd finished early for the day. Instead of heading straight to the house, I'd taken Steve's advice and booked an appointment with the GP, certain that she was going to prove him wrong. Instead, she knocked me for six.

"Congratulations," she told me. "You're expecting!"

"Really?!" I gasped. "I had no idea!"

She paused for a moment as though she was struggling to find the right words.

"Is something wrong?" I asked.

"It's just that I think you're probably a little bit further along than you might imagine."

"How much further along?"

"Well – more than half way."

My jaw hit the floor. This makes me sound really dippy, I know, but I hadn't had a clue – and now I was going to be a mum in a little over four months' time!

Back at home, I waited for Steve to land from work before breaking the news.

"I can't believe it!" he thrilled. "I'm going to be a dad!"

"Yes, sooner than you think, actually," I told him.

Steve's brow creased in puzzlement. "How do you mean?"

"Well – the doctor reckons I'm already nearly five months gone," I said. "I mean – what am I going to tell work?"

For a second, he looked gobsmacked. But Steve was unflappable. "Never mind work," he told me, clapping his hands together. "We'd better get our skates on!"

The very next day, we bundled into the car – full of nervous excitement – and drove out to Merry Hill shopping centre in Brierley Hill, where there was a huge baby shop. We filled the boot with baby clothes, toys and nappies, and just had room to squeeze in a Moses basket.

"Let's stop off at Mum and Dad's on the way home and break the news," I said.

Steve agreed.

After knocking on their door I led my bewildered-looking mum and dad back to the car. Steve popped the boot open and I said proudly: "Look what we've bought today!"

"Oh, that's nice," said Mum. "Which one of your friends is having a baby?"

"No! It's for us," I said. "You're going to be a grandma!"

Mum gasped. "I'd given up hope. Come here," she said and pulled me in for a hug. She and Dad were over the moon.

We got the same reaction from Steve's parents. Our baby was going to be the first grandchild on both sides. "I was starting to think you might never have children," said Madge. Her face lit up and she cupped my face in her hands, kissing me on the forehead. "Bless you," she said.

The next few months flew by. Steve and I were both dead excited about the impending new arrival, and as everyone convinced us we were having a boy, we had a list of boys' names, with Luke or Harrison the favourites.

"Put Tarquin on the list," said Steve.

"Tarquin? You're having me on."

"No, I really like it," he said, looking away and trying to hide a smile.

That became Steve's little wind-up whenever we got together with family.

"Yeah, we're thinking 'Tarquin'," Steve would announce, stunning everyone into awkward silence.

Even though we still carried on like big kids sometimes, we were more than ready for parenthood. We'd done everything we wanted to, and felt now was the right time. Sure, we could have started a family when we were younger – but that would have meant missing out on all those fun times you have in your 20s. Instead, we'd got all that out of the way and now had more time, energy and money to put into family life.

For the most part, my extra-short pregnancy was a breeze. I got accustomed to the whiff of greasy beef burgers, which bizarrely seemed to follow me around wherever I went. And Steve got used to satisfying my nocturnal craving for Calippo ice lollies. I thought nothing of digging an elbow in Steve's ribs to nudge him awake in the middle of the night.

"All right! All right! I'm going," he'd say, stumbling out of bed and then driving from one 24-hour garage to the next on a lolly search mission.

One thing I *didn't* get used to was being messed about with by medical staff. And – in particular – medical staff armed with hypodermic needles. Steve and I started going to National Childbirth Trust Classes during the pregnancy, so I could get some reassurance about what lay ahead, as well as some advice about avoiding my needle phobia by having a natural childbirth. Steve wanted to be involved as much as possible in the birth and listened intently, following the midwife's instructions for natural pain relief by massaging my neck, back and forehead.

Still, going for antenatal appointments was a nightmare. Because I'd fainted before at the sight of a hypodermic, I gave the nurse advance warning on one surgery visit.

"I'm not good with needles," I told her. "I've got a proper phobia."

She was an old-fashioned, matronly sort who clearly didn't suffer fools gladly. She had me marked down as one right away, and a little smile crept into one corner of her mouth, as if to say, *Yeah, yeah. Heard it all before.*

This time, I'd brought Steve along for back-up in case I had another funny turn. He must have caught the look on her face as he intervened: "She really is scared of needles."

"You'll be fine, dear," the midwife said, walking towards me with a syringe in her hand. "We'll just take some bloods – if you could roll your sleeve up for me, please."

That's all it took. The room seemed to spin sideways. My vision dimmed to grey then blacked out completely as my legs folded underneath me. The next thing I knew I was coming to on the examination couch with a crowd of people around me.

"Are you alright, love?" Steve said, taking my hand.

Instinctively, I stroked my baby bump.

"I think so," I stammered.

"You were out cold. We had to grab some lads from the waiting room to lift you off the floor."

"I'm very sorry, Mrs Williams," the midwife said.

Steve tutted at her. "It's not like we didn't warn you!"

While I was pregnant, whenever Steve was out on patrol with the Specials, he called home to check in with me. "Everything okay? Are you alright? Do you need me to come back?"

"No, I'm fine!" I'd tell him. "You carry on."

Then one evening as my due date got near, Steve was booked in for a night shift. But in the meantime, there was the small matter of Telford United vs Stoke in the FA Cup.

"I'll go and see Mum and Dad while you're at the match," I suggested.

It was a cold November day. Steve dropped me off at theirs on the way to the ground, and waved goodbye as I waddled up their garden path, bump stuck out in front of me like the side of a house. It was only then I realised I hadn't bothered to check ahead to see if they'd be in. And after knocking on the door, my heart sank – I was met with silence. *You'll just have to wait*, I grumbled, using the porch for support as I lowered myself to the floor and parked my behind on the doorstep. As the time passed, I squirmed uncomfortably, trying to ward off the chill creeping into my bones. On its tail came sporadic twists of pain in my tummy. *Mind over matter*, I told myself, pushing them away. *Just breathe.*

It was a good two or three hours before Mum and Dad showed up, and by then I was sure I was in the first stages of labour, no doubt sparked by an afternoon spent freezing my backside off sat on their cold doorstep.

They busied me inside, full of apologies, and I slumped on the sofa. Going by my watch, I was looking at another couple of hours' wait before Steve showed up.

I hope they don't go into extra time, I thought, fidgeting about and trying to get comfortable.

Mum flashed me a look. "Are you OK?" she said. "You seem awfully quiet."

"Yes, I'm all right, Mum. Don't worry."

"Is the baby wriggling? You can't sit still!"

"Yes, that's what it is," I said, with a thin-lipped smile. I just wanted to be at home. But for the time being I had to tough it out.

Steve finally showed up about half five.

"Good game, Steve?" my dad began.

"Nil nil," Steve huffed, undoing his coat.

"Let me get that," Dad said. "Do you want a cup of tea?"

Steve was about to reply when I struggled to my feet. "Actually I think we'll get going," I said, flashing Steve a look to let him know I meant it.

In the car on the way home, I told him: "I think it's starting."

"Now?"

"At Mum's. The last few hours have been a nightmare."

"Do we need to go to the hospital?"

"No, just get me home," I said. "I want my own space."

By now, my 'twinges' had set into a regular cycle. Steve was due at the station but didn't know what to do with himself.

"What do you think? Shall I go in?" he asked.

"Of course!" I said, waving him away. "Don't worry."

"Alright. But let me run you a bath first."

As Steve set off for work, I sank into the warm water. By now, my 'twinges' were growing in intensity. The bath helped soothe the pain a little and, afterwards, I tried once more to push it to the back of my mind.

But really, I was only delaying the inevitable. My baby was coming.

Tonight.

When Steve's usual call didn't come, I picked up the phone and dialled the station. Everyone there knew our situation and the woman in the control room was bursting with excitement for us.

"I'll put out a call for him, Lynnette," she said. "Hang on!"

"I'll do my best – but tell him not to drag his feet," I said, gasping as another wave of pain rolled through me.

Steve was out on patrol in one of the vans when the radio crackled into life. "We have a message for Special Constable Williams – your wife needs you at home."

And this night – of all nights – Steve had a brain freeze. "OK. Do you know why?" he asked.

Barely missing a beat, the radio operator said: "We shouldn't really need to tell you why, but she did insist you go pretty quick!"

"Oh! Yes – of course!" Steve said, slapping his forehead.

His colleagues got him back to the station in double quick time and he drove home to find me puffing and panting, wearing a groove in the hall carpet as I paced up and down.

"Come on, let's get you in the car," he said.

I shook my head. "I'm not going in yet. They'll just start poking and prodding me. I don't want to be messed with," I said, waving him over. "Come here, I need some fresh air. Help me outside will you?"

Steve took my arm and walked me up and down the driveway as I did my breathing exercises. Finally, when I couldn't stand it any longer, I said to him: "All right – I think we'd better get going."

Steve rang the hospital and spoke to the midwife. I saw him shake his head and say: "No – we're coming in now!"

Then he hung up. "She wanted us to wait another hour," he said, helping me into the car.

"No chance," I huffed.

As Steve drove to the old Wrekin Maternity Hospital, I remember telling him: "Can't you go any quicker!?"

Maybe he was steadfastly observing the speed limit, because it wouldn't do for a Special to get caught speeding, but this baby really didn't care much for 30mph zones. "I don't think I can hold on much longer!" I winced through gritted teeth as I lay across the back seat of the car.

The hospital was an old, Victorian red brick building with cold corridors and walls lined with faded tiles.

"It's your first isn't it?" the midwife commented, as if to say, *get settled in – you're going to be a while yet.* But she soon changed her tune after examining me. "OK. We'd better find you a room right away," she said.

With my fear of needles, I turned down an epidural and pressed ahead with my natural birth plan. Steve diligently kneaded my neck and back, putting into practice the techniques he'd learned from the NCT. But when I couldn't stand it any longer I flipped on him like the little girl in *The Exorcist.* "Stop bloody rubbing my back!" I hissed, eyes blazing.

Steve didn't need telling twice, and quietly retreated to the other end of the bed.

Not long later – just an hour after we'd arrived – I delivered our baby.

"Oh – you've got a little girl!" the midwife said.

"No," I said. "I'm having a boy."

"It's definitely a girl!"

"Really!" I said, ecstatic. "It's a girl!" We named her Scarlett.

Back then, they kept you in hospital for days after giving birth. It felt like forever and I couldn't wait to get home, away from the draughty, single-glazed windows and miserable little showers.

"We need to keep you in for rest," the nurse told me as I fed my new daughter.

Stop blimmin' well waking me up every five minutes to ask if I'm OK then, I thought.

Eventually, after about five days, I was finally allowed home to chill out with the new one. During the day, Scarlett was a little angel. I could take her anywhere, she never cried. She was just a lovely, funny baby.

At night, we put her to sleep in the Moses basket on Steve's side of the bed. She insisted on having his hand in her cot, and she'd close a tiny fist around one of his fingers. Often, even that failed to soothe her and when her wailing got too much, Steve strapped her into her car seat and motored far out into the countryside hoping the drive would work some special magic that we'd failed to conjure. Scarlett fought it for as long as she could hold out, the mileometer ticking ever upwards and the needle on the fuel gauge slumping down. Maybe it was the hum of the tyres on the road that lulled her into sleep, or the gentle bump and sway of the suspension. Eventually, her little eyelids drooped and then fell heavily over her baby blue eyes. Steve drove back to the house on tenterhooks, expecting Scarlett to wake up any minute and start wailing once more – but those eyes stayed tightly shut all the way home. She was still fast asleep as he turned into our street, still dreaming as he parked up on our drive, still sleeping peacefully as he tugged on the handbrake – and then he turned the engine off. As soon as its soothing purr stopped, Scarlett jolted awake, filled those lungs and began to scream!

In other ways, Scarlett was a hilarious baby, a bundle of infectious giggles who loved blowing huge raspberries. We bought a baby bouncer which hung from the living room door frame, and Scarlett set herself the challenge of trying to chase us while she was still strapped into it. She'd only get so far before the laws of physics came into play – the springs recoiled, lifting her feet clean off the ground, and she'd ping backwards, shrieking with laughter. We'd laugh along with her and our own giggles would fuel even more from Scarlett.

She was a quick learner in many respects, and took her first steps at just ten months old. We'd been for a break in Manorbier in Pembrokeshire, and on the day we set off back home it was my birthday. On the way, we stopped at a toy shop and bought a little push-along horse. Scarlett had started to cruise around the living room, pulling herself upright by the side of the settee and clinging to furniture as she toddled about. We thought the horse would bring her on and give her the confidence to take her first proper steps.

We got home and started unloading the car. While I disappeared into the bedroom, Steve propped Scarlett up beside the settee.

I was only gone a second when I heard him call: "Lynnette – she's walking! She's walking!"

I went running down to see and, sure enough, there she was stumbling towards her dad. Steve was grinning from ear to ear. "Well that horse was a waste of £35!" he joked. It didn't matter. Seeing our little girl take her first steps was the best birthday present ever.

I soon got back to work in Boots as a job share manager. I loved the social side of it, and getting a discount on baby things was a big bonus. I did 12 hours – two short days a week – and the grandparents shared looking after Scarlett while I was in work.

Steve was still loving his weekends with the Specials and he made it known at the station that he had his eye on a bigger prize – his aim was to get into the regulars. His knack for the job hadn't gone unnoticed among his superiors – in those days, it was rare for Specials to put in their own files for court, but within a short space of time, if they had an arrest, Steve was given the extra responsibility of pulling the paperwork together for the prosecution. Specials often got ridiculed for being 'hobby bobbies', but it was no idle pastime for Steve. He did it all by the letter. Just like in the day job, he was precise and diligent.

Sometimes, he couldn't help bringing the job home with him – like the time we were living on a tough estate while we waited on a move to a new house. Scarlett was about 18 months old and I'd bought a doer-upper on a whim. It was a tatty old bungalow in Rindleford near Bridgnorth, tucked away down a little track, next door to an old waterboard pumping station. I'd gone to view it one day while Steve was working away. With no electricity and boarded-up windows, I followed the estate agent around in semi-darkness, the beam of her torchlight picking out peeling wallpaper and taps jutting from walls on lengths of copper pipe. But, despite the mess, I saw the potential – and was certain Steve would, too. I walked out, called Steve and told him: "We've bought it!"

It needed some work before we could safely let toddler Scarlett loose inside. In the meantime we were renting a house on this estate in Telford. Having put in the hours in the Specials, Steve was clued up on all the local crime hotspots, and – as we were temporarily living in one – he'd bought an alarm for the company car.

One night, we were lying in bed just about to drift off to sleep when the alarm burst into life, jolting us wide awake. Steve sat bolt upright and said: "That's our car!" Without a stitch of clothing on – he leapt out of bed, swept down the stairs and snatched my leather jacket from the bannister, pulling it on as he headed for the front door. Outside, he found three lads loitering around the car, which for the time being was concealing Steve's modesty.

"What are you lot doing?" Steve asked.

"We're just walking home from the club," one piped up.

"You weren't trying to break into this car were you?"

As the lads backed away, Steve walked round the car, so hyped up that he was completely oblivious to how he was dressed. These lads took one look, then set off running down the road.

"Oy!" Steve yelled after them, shaking a fist, before he came stomping back in the house.

I looked him up and down, gobsmacked. "Have you seen yourself?" I said. It hadn't even registered to Steve that he was wearing my waist-length leather coat – and nothing else.

We were in no rush to add to our brood, so for the next four years, Scarlett got our undivided attention. I'd take her on walks, we did arts and crafts together – painting, drawing and making little models. It dawned on me one day, when I was covered up to my elbows in poster paint and glue, that I'd finally grown up and settled down!

Scarlett's curiosity about the world around her fed into a love of nature, and once she sussed out my fear of creepy crawlies, she'd wind me up by putting worms and woodlice in her pockets for me to find.

The concept of shyness didn't exist for Scarlett, so she quickly gained a big circle of friends. Even when she was a little dot she was forever having mates around on play dates. She was just as uninhibited with grown-ups, toddling up to total strangers to announce: "My name Tardy." She couldn't say her name at first, so Tardy it was. We still call her that today.

And she had a mischievous streak to her. At three years old, she'd go and find Steve washing the car, pick up the hose and give him a soaking. Later, when she started at the local infant school, the teacher took me aside one day at home time.

"If you could just have a little chat with Scarlett," she said.

"What's happened?" I asked.

"I had to pop out of the classroom for a couple of minutes and asked them all to quietly get on with their work. Only when I came back, all the kids had vanished."

It turned out the staff had discovered a fire door wide open. Scarlett had instigated a mass exodus by suggesting to her classmates they all go for a walk to the bluebell forest while the teacher was away.

All this time, Steve was still mulling over whether to quit his job and go into policing full time. He loved the idea that it was a different role every day, that he never really knew what he was going to have to deal with until he was there, right in the moment. Gordon was full of enthusiasm, while still being honest about the good and the bad sides of working for the police full time.

"It'll mean some changes," Steve said. "We've got used to a certain lifestyle and it's not going to be the same money coming in."

But I thought we could deal with it. I had no qualms. OK, it was going to be a hit on the money. But that didn't matter – we'd got to a stage in our lives where we'd done the stuff we wanted to do, and we were never frightened of tightening our belts and just knuckling down. With a little one to look after, it's not like we were out every weekend eating and drinking. And money wasn't everything.

"We'll live on beans on toast," I shrugged. "If you want to do it – go for it."

I wasn't worried at all. I knew he'd be a good fit for the job, because nothing flustered him. I was sure joining the police would give him a new lease of life and – worst case scenario – if he ended up hating it, he'd soon land another job back in industry.

It was decided. Gordon filled Steve in on the interview process and gave him tips on what the police were looking for. In October

1994, when Scarlett was four years old, Steve put his application in for the regulars. He was invited to take part in a selection weekend and, by the end of it, was told he'd got the job. He officially joined up in February the following year, starting on his basic police training.

In those days, it was a long drawn-out affair involving on-the-job training at a local police station, and ten weeks away at the cadet college down in Cwmbran, South Wales. Steve hadn't long started when I noticed once more that swollen feeling in my belly. It was like a replay of my first pregnancy four years earlier. The GP confirmed it. I was expecting again and – just as before – we wouldn't have long to wait. I was already several months gone. We were both thrilled.

"But I don't want to bugger off on training and leave you," Steve said.

"Don't be daft. I can manage," I told him. "I'm not an invalid. And anyway, by the time this one's due you should be back on placement at the station."

The dates worked. By the time Steve set off to Cwmbran, I had just over ten weeks to go. Perfect.

Almost perfect.

The time flew by, but on my 35th birthday and with two weeks of training left to go, I began to feel the familiar twinges of my labour beginning. It was a Thursday evening and Steve arrived home for the weekend, setting down a pile of papers to revise for exams the following week.

"How you feeling, love?" he asked me.

He'd barely had time to take his coat off when I patted my bulge and nodded: "I think it's happening."

"Do we need to go?" he said. After our experience with Scarlett he knew I wasn't messing around.

But I was determined to leave it until the last possible minute. "I'll hang on a bit."

Eventually, I couldn't hold on any longer. After dropping Scarlett with my mum, we headed to the hospital, arriving just before midnight. A stressed-looking midwife busied out to see us and said: "We'll see if we can find a room – we're full at the moment. And as you've only just started having contractions…"

Steve stopped her. "If my wife says she's having this baby, it means she's having this baby," he said. "And soon, so I suggest you find a bed for her!"

There really was no room at the inn, so a nurse put me in a storage room at the back of the hospital, wedged in between a spare wheelchair and racking filled with old bed pans.

When the midwife came to check on me, she tutted and said: "We'll kick someone out and get you straight through."

And so, Georgia, like Scarlett, arrived really quickly – within an hour. She was born at 1.05am on Friday September 8th 1995.

Now – besides Scarlett – we had a new baby to juggle, plus Steve's impending end-of-course tests. He rang in on the Monday and asked: "Can I have a couple of extra days, just so my wife can recuperate?"

"As long as you're back here for 9am on Wednesday morning for all your exams," they told him.

On the day, he got up at 5am and drove to South Wales to finish the course. Six weeks later, we returned as a family for Steve's passing out parade. Watching him march up and down in his constable's uniform was such a proud moment for me. I had Georgia, just six weeks old – literally a babe in arms – clutched to my chest. Scarlett – a few weeks off turning five – was beside me.

"Can you see Daddy?" I said to her.

She pointed into the throng of newly qualified officers. "Daddy's a policeman!"

He wasn't hard to spot – Steve was the oldest among a bunch of fresh-faced young officers. But age didn't matter. *He's going to be a blimmin' good one,* I thought. Later that evening, at the passing out parade black tie ball, I found myself wiping away a tear as Steve stood up in front of everyone and gave a speech on behalf of all the new recruits. He had everyone in stitches with funny stories from their months of training. I was certain he was going to be an asset to the police. He'd worked so hard to get in, and he had such high morals and high standards in everything he did, I knew he'd carry that through into his new job.

It's just a shame, a tragedy, that not all officers shared the same values. I couldn't possibly have known then how, one day, it would end up costing Georgia – my babe in arms – her life.

TWO

Georgia lay in her basket, gurgling softly, exuding calm. It barely seemed possible that Scarlett – with her nerve-shredding, ear-piercing scream – could have come from the same womb as her older sister. They were like chalk and cheese in that respect. Or – as friends and family liked to say – Scarlett was pink and Georgia was blue.

"She's so chilled!" I remarked to Steve when Georgia was just a few weeks old, letting go a sigh of relief. "I can't believe it."

"I barely know she's there half the time," he said.

As long as Georgia was fed, she was happy, and she soon filled out into a gorgeous, chubby baby with soft, plump cheeks and a round tummy. "She's like a little Weeble," I said one day, watching her wobbling away as she tried to stay sitting upright.

"She wobbles all right, but she doesn't fall down!" laughed Steve.

As the months went by, Georgia's laid-back approach to life seeped into everything she did – or rather *didn't* – do. She was in no rush to burn off any of that baby fat – learning to crawl or even roll over from her back onto her tum was just far too much effort. Sometimes I'd catch Scarlett spreadeagled on the floor next to her sister. "Like this…" she'd say, arms and legs pumping as she crawled across the carpet. "Come on – you try." But Georgia just stared contentedly at her, lying on her belly and steadfastly refusing to budge from her playmat, as if to say, "I don't need to crawl when I've got you." She had her sussed – she knew she just had to bide her time and Scarlett would run and fetch her whatever she wanted.

Unlike her big sister, Georgia was in no hurry to take her first steps, either, but she did get there eventually, toddling around in a dream world of her own, palms pressed to her favourite trundle-along car, squirrelling stuff away in the boot as she went. It was a treasure trove of missing objects – whenever I couldn't find something I always knew where to look first. Another favourite game was dressing up poor Muttley, our long-suffering Shitzu dog, in old baby clothes. We'd got him as a puppy for Scarlett's fifth birthday, and Muttley was that daft and soppy that he let them do it. Squeezed into a white babygrow or looking like a cream puff in a frilly dress, he'd sit in their toy pram with his tongue hanging out while they took turns parading him around the house.

By three years old, while other kids her age were proper chatterboxes, Georgia kept her words and thoughts locked away, as though she was still compiling the vocabulary for what she wanted to say. I raised it at check-ups but as long as Georgia was healthy and happy, they were never unduly worried. "It'll come when she's ready," they advised me.

Still, at bed times, she was no trouble at all. Often, we'd be watching TV in the evening while the girls sat freshly bathed and glowing in their pyjamas, thumbing through one of their favourite picture books, and Georgia would suddenly take herself off down the hall to her bedroom. She'd look back at me with a smile and say: "Night night! Bed time!"

She didn't *always* stay there, though. One night in the wee hours, I was fast asleep in bed when I suddenly snapped wide awake with a start. That unnerving sensation that you're not alone had slithered into my dreams. I felt a warm breath tickle my cheek, and once my eyes adjusted to the gloom I saw Georgia's pale face glowing in the darkness an inch from mine, lips mumbling unintelligibly. Another time, Steve got up bleary-eyed to go to the loo and opened our bedroom door to find Georgia stood there – stock still – staring blankly into space. Steve jumped back in fright.

"She scared me half to death!" he told me the next morning.

For a few years, Georgia's unsettling 'night terrors' became a regular occurrence. A consultant advised she'd grow out of them eventually, but in the meantime all we could do was gently walk her back to bed, reassuring her that she was safe.

"Is everything OK?" I asked Georgia one day. "Are you having bad dreams?"

She looked at me and nodded solemnly.

"Do you want to tell me what they're about?"

I felt a shiver run down my spine as she replied ominously: "You wouldn't want to know."

Later, I told Steve.

"There's something very spiritual about that one," he said.

I knew what he was getting at. Georgia had an imaginary friend for a while and I'd often catch her staring away into the corner of the room as though she was talking to someone, or something.

Other times, Georgia was quick-witted and down to earth, with a dry sense of humour that left us rocking on our heels. She was five when we hired a huge bouncy castle for her birthday, and a clown to entertain all the kids when they were done running themselves ragged. After we'd sent all her little friends on their way with a party bag and a slice of cake, one of Steve's workmates – John Walker – called by the house on his way home from work.

"Hello Georgia!" he said. "Did you enjoy your birthday party?"

"Yes I did," she beamed.

"I hear you had a special guest," John replied.

"Yes, I had a clown."

"And what was he dressed like?" John asked.

Without missing a beat, Georgia told him straight: "Like a clown of course!"

She had us in stitches. Laughing, John slapped his forehead. "I've just realised what a stupid question that was!" he said.

As well as us adults, Georgia soon learned which buttons to press to wind her sister up, too. And by winding her up, I mean frightening her half to death. Scarlett got a kick out of giving me a scare by hiding worms and bugs in my pockets, but her love of creepy crawlies didn't stretch to spiders. If Scarlett got stroppy with Georgia in some way, or perhaps didn't want to play with her for whatever reason, Georgia would present her cupped hands as though she was hiding something inside. "I don't think you'd like what I've got in here!" Or she'd feign shock and tell Scarlett: "Have you seen what's crawling up your back?"

Sometimes, if Scarlett had really annoyed her, she'd go even further. One night the girls were getting tucked up in bed ready for lights out when we heard Scarlett screaming: "Dad! Dad! There's a spider!" And between her screams, coming from Georgia's bedroom, we caught the sound of hysterical laughter. It was no accident that this eight-legged intruder had suddenly shown up on Scarlett's bedroom wall!

Since joining the police, Steve was like a totally different bloke. He left for work each day with a spring in his step. The job had given him back his spark – and still left him plenty of time for dad duties. Shift work, when Steve was in uniform, suited family life to a tee. It meant he was there for the girls while I was doing my two days co-managing Boots. Having a policeman dad was a thrill for them, too. They were always excited to see him come home in his smart uniform, greeting him with: "Did you get to chase anybody today, Dad?"

"Not today, girls," Steve told them one evening. "We were far too busy for chasing baddies."

"What did you do?" they chorused. "Tell us!"

"Well – downstairs underneath the station we've got an alien spaceship and we're taking it in turns to guard it!"

Poor girls. They believed every word.

It was the same at Christmas, when Steve used to dress up as Santa and we'd arrange it so the girls would spot him from their bedroom window, a sack of presents slung across his back.

Scarlett clung to those memories at least until secondary school, and at 12 years old she was still telling classmates she knew Father Christmas was real because she'd seen him. She'd chosen Ercall Wood Technology College after primary. Not long after she started, I was at parents' evening with her, sat in a classroom listening to one of the teachers. Behind us was a young girl with long blonde hair and an attractive face. As she chatted away with Scarlett, I found myself warming to her. She was so open and friendly, and something about the way she and Scarlett were with each other told me they were going to be in each other's lives for years to come.

"Who's that?" I asked Scarlett later. "She seems really nice."

"She's called Jadine. Jadine Dunning," Scarlett told me. "I was going to ask – can she come for tea one day?"

The girls' friends were always welcome. "Course she can," I said.

A few days later, I found myself juggling frozen pizzas while Jadine and Scarlett belted out Disney songs up in her bedroom. They even let Georgia – the annoying kid sister – in on the act. *I don't know how she stands it,* I pondered as I set the table for the three of them. *They think they can sing but they're both tone blimmin' deaf.*

In no time, Jadine became almost like a third daughter to us. I calmed her nerves when she sat on the plane to Portugal hyperventilating with fear, terrified of flying, as we took her on holiday. She joined me on the sofa watching romcoms with the girls while Steve was out on night shifts. I dished out advice when Scarlett came to me, worried that Jadine – still only 13 – was out of her depth with an older boyfriend. I never shied away from these difficult conversations. At work in Boots, I was known among the Saturday girls as a mother hen they could confide in if they'd got themselves into some bother over a boy. Some of the stories they came out with – very little made me blush.

"Will you have a word with Jadine, Mum?" Scarlett said. "She's seeing this lad and I'm not sure about him."

"Not sure?"

"He's older. And he's pushy, you know what I mean?"

"I do."

Scarlett was at a loss. "I've tried saying to her, Mum, but she won't listen to me. Will you have a go?"

One Sunday morning after a sleepover we were sat in the conservatory munching on bacon butties when Scarlett gave me the nod.

"You know – us girls, we should treasure our bodies. Honour them," I said. Scarlett was well used to this kind of chat, but I thought Jadine might run a mile but she stopped mid-chew and listened. "You know what I'm on about, don't you?"

"Yeah."

"Think about it, Jadine. This boy – he's obviously a man of the world already. And some boys, the way they look at girls – the way they treat them – it can be wrong."

I think any other child would have told me where to go, but somehow I'd struck a chord. She nodded. "Thanks Lynnette."

* * *

Very quickly, after just three years as a uniformed police officer, Steve became a plain clothes detective. It was a bittersweet moment because he'd had his sights set on a detective role for years, and on the day of his interview we got the devastating news that his mum had passed away. Within the week we learned he'd got the job. Madge would have been so proud.

It was a few years later, when Georgia was maybe five or six, that we stood watching her from the kitchen window as she played on the swing in the garden. She cocked her head from side to side and nodded up and down, chatting away as though she was deep in conversation with somebody. Somebody who wasn't there. She was completely alone.

"What's she doing?" Steve said, baffled.

I shrugged. "It must be that imaginary friend again."

When Georgia tired of the swing, she came trotting in the house.

"All right, Georgia?" Steve said. "Who were you chatting with then?"

She blinked back at him. "I've been talking to nanny Madge."

We were both dumbstruck.

Georgia had only been a toddler when Madge had passed, too young to really cotton on to her name. It was so strange.

The girls and I slotted easily into a routine based around whatever shifts Steve was working. Usually it was regular office hours – Monday to Friday – but if they had a case to crack he'd tumble in at one in the morning and be up and out again by five. The girls knew when to pull their weight so we weren't scurrying around the house like headless chickens on school mornings. Driving them to school, radio blasting as we sang along to a Steps CD, was a joy. They were never any trouble for me.

Steve earned a reputation for having a firm but fair approach – and not just from his CID colleagues. I remember one time out shopping, stood in B&Q waiting for the till with the girls on one side of me, and Steve on the other. A face pushed through among the other shoppers, made eye contact with Steve, and came over. He was a big guy, tall and well built, rolls of wallpaper tucked under one arm.

Do I know him? I was thinking, as he greeted Steve with a warm smile.

"All right? How you getting on?" I heard the man say to Steve.

"Not bad at all," Steve told him.

There was a bit of friendly small talk while I put our shopping through the till, and then the man headed off. He'd looked genuinely pleased to see Steve.

I was curious. "Who's that then?" I said, as we walked to the car.

"Oh – somebody I sent to prison on a job."

"Oh my God!" I gasped.

"No, it's fine," Steve reassured me. "He's OK with me. He understands I had to nick him, but I was fair with him and treated him with respect."

That kind of thing happened a few times when we were out and about, because Steve was committed to dealing with criminals even-handedly. It was something we always tried to instil in the girls as well – that same standard of dealing with people – showing respect, not bearing grudges, giving folk a second chance. Both the girls took it on board, Georgia especially, in a way that was actually heartbreaking.

With five years between the girls, while Scarlett was progressing through secondary school, Georgia was still in primary. She was in Year 4 when she came home one day with red, bloody grazes scuffing her knees and flecks of gravel buried in her palms.

"What happened here, love?" I asked her.

Georgia slumped, looking crestfallen for a moment, before brushing it off. "I just fell over in the playground," she said. "I'm OK though."

A few bumps and bruises from the rough and tumble of the playground were inevitable, and Georgia always took them in her stride. She was only slight, but she was a toughie in that way. I wouldn't have thought any more of it, but as the weeks and months went by, these scuffs and bruises became an all too regular occurrence. She'd come home covered in grazes, with chunks of skin torn from her palms where she'd tried to break her fall. Each time, Georgia's explanation was the same: She'd tripped. She'd stumbled. She'd fallen.

"Maybe there's something wrong with her," I suggested to Steve, thinking perhaps her balance was out of whack. "I'd best take her to the doctor."

"Better safe than sorry," he said. "She has been quiet, hasn't she? Have you noticed?"

Georgia hadn't been her usual bright self for a while. I was determined to get to the bottom of what was going on.

The GP was none the wiser and she referred Georgia to the local hospital. Even there – after a round of examinations and blood tests – the consultant was at a loss. "Her balance and reflexes are fine," he said. "The only thing I can think of is that perhaps her muscles are still developing and it's affected her co-ordination."

"Is there anything we can do?" I asked.

"It's probably something she'll grow out of."

Only she didn't grow out of it. Instead – as each new bruise flowered on her knees and elbows – Georgia became more and more timid. I asked and asked her what the problem was, but she would never let on.

The last straw came just as we were about to head for a half term holiday to Lanzarote. We saved up all year for holidays, and went away whenever the kids were off school. Steve always banked a load of overtime so we had the extra cash. It was important, quality family time for us. Memory making.

On this occasion, Steve went to pick her up from school while I finished off packing and when they got home my jaw hit the ground.

Georgia's face was covered in grazes – she looked like she had third degree burns.

"Georgia, sweetheart!" I said, my heart breaking for her. "Whatever happened?"

But she just shrugged timidly and said, "Fell over again."

Steve looked at me, at a loss, as if to say *What do we do?*

Later, as we stood in the check-in queue at the airport, I caught strangers staring at our Georgia. I couldn't deny it – she looked terrible. I just had to hope they didn't think we'd done it to her.

In Spain, Georgia wore a wide-brimmed hat to shield her wounds from the scorching sun. They must have stung like crazy when she went in the water, but she was like a fish – you couldn't keep her out of the pool or the sea. While we were on holiday, I went out of my way to butter her up but it wasn't until we were back home that I finally managed to coax out of her what was going on at school. Georgia broke down in floods of tears, shoulders heaving as she stammered between sobs: "I keep getting pushed, I keep getting bullied."

By now, it had been going on the best part of two years. I felt awful for her. It cut me to the core. You hate to think of your child suffering when you're not there to protect them. You drop them off at school expecting them to be safe, not in pain. And all this time, she'd been suffering in silence. Like her sister, Georgia wouldn't have hurt a fly. Quite the opposite – both girls would stand up for others.

"Who was it?" I asked. "You can tell us."

But Georgia shook her head. She wouldn't name names at first. All I knew was that they were ganging up on her in the playground.

Steve and I saw red. We couldn't get our heads around how it had gone on for so long without anyone intervening. What were the dinner ladies, teachers and playground monitors doing?

I thought a move to a new school might be the best solution for Georgia. "We can find somewhere new for you," I suggested.

But she was strong-willed and adamant. "No – I love it there. I love the teachers. And I'm not going to let them push me out. I just don't want to be bullied anymore."

We decided to let Georgia handle things her way. In any case, in another 12 months or so, she'd be moving up to secondary. We had a decision to make about where she went next.

"She seems to like Scarlett's school," Steve said.

It was true. She'd been to a few shows and events at Ercall Wood, and she was leaning towards following in her big sister's footsteps. We already knew it was a good school – and there was an added bonus: It was out of catchment, on the other side of Wellington, and therefore an unlikely choice for most of Georgia's classmates. Bullies included.

"I don't think I could stand it if she ended up in the same school as those girls," I said. "I wouldn't be able to rest."

We just needed to push it over the line. Maybe it was time for another move.

Steve asked around at work. "Turns out quite a few from the station live around there. They seem to think it's a nice area," he said.

We drove over for a look around. Wellington was still close enough to Telford, but the rolling Shropshire Hills were right on the doorstep, with the familiar, volcano-like mound of the Wrekin just a stone's throw to the south of the town centre. In the estate agents, one house leapt out at me. It was a 1950s detached, the sort of place that would always turn Madge's head. "That's the kind of house I'd like to live in," she'd say. It had four bedrooms, with a nice bit of land around it, decent gardens front and back, and was just over the road from a lovely park. Plus, the secondary school wasn't too far away.

It ticked all the boxes for Steve and me.

The girls, though? They weren't so keen.

"What do you think?" I asked them as the estate agent showed us around.

"Please, Mum. No!" Georgia said, grimacing at the ancient kitchen. It was a nightmare of tarnished 60s Formica and sliding cupboard doors. "Look at it!"

Paper doilies lined the shelves, trailing dusty frills. "What are they?" Scarlett said, pulling a face and pointing. "Ugh!"

But we saw the potential, and we really thought we were doing right by the girls by moving to a decent area.

They say you never know what dangers might be lurking around the corner. We honestly thought we were moving our family – moving Georgia – to a place of safety. How wrong we were.

THREE

Georgia slapped a palm against the rough cardboard of a removal box. "This one's for my room!" she announced. "Mum!"

"Hang on, I'm coming now!" I said. The new house was a chaos of furniture and packing crates. We'd eventually won Scarlett's grudging approval by promising her the bigger of the two kids' bedrooms. Those awful paper doilies were long gone from the kitchen. The big move was on.

I clambered over the obstacle course of cardboard littering the hallway. As I stooped to grab Georgia's box of toys, a folded slip of paper on the floor below the letterbox caught my eye.

Reading the note, I said to Georgia: "Actually, I think this one's for you."

"What does it say?"

"It says, I've heard there's a little girl the same age as me moving into the street," I read. "It would be really nice if we could be friends."

It was signed 'Tabitha', in spidery handwriting, along with a house number. She lived a few doors away. "What do you think?" I asked Georgia.

She beamed excitedly. "Can I go and see her?"

"Now?"

Georgia nodded.

"Let's just shift some of these boxes first," I said. "Here, you grab that one."

Later, when the house had at least a semblance of order, I took Georgia to meet her new playmate. Tabitha was a bright, wholesome kid with cheery parents. Her mum taught piano and she was thrilled to hear Georgia was learning keyboard. Art and craft stuff covered the dining room table and Georgia wasted no time getting stuck in alongside her new friend. With everything going on at school, it was comforting to see Georgia playing with someone she felt so at home with.

The two girls became inseparable. Georgia would go up to Tabitha's to practise piano and eat home-cooked food like cauliflower cheese and spaghetti bolognaise. Tabitha came to ours for rare treats of freezer junk – chicken nuggets and pizzas – plus a dose of Xbox adrenaline. Steve would take them to the park, scaring them silly by pushing them higher and higher on the swings until they were practically horizontal. They called it 'The Swing of Doom', and it made them scream with fear and excitement in equal measure. In quieter moments, the girls were just content in each other's company, playing out on our driveway, or parked on the kerb in the late afternoon sun, striking up chit-chat with passing neighbours. At Halloween, I joined Tabitha's mum taking the girls trick-or-treating round our cul-de-sac. Everyone on the street got to know them. We felt safe and sheltered. Surrounded by neighbours who looked out for the girls, I couldn't contemplate anything bad visiting our corner of Wellington.

Away from school, Georgia was relaxed and happy. But in the bear pit of the break-time playground, she was still getting stick from a small band of troublemakers. Gently, over time, we prised some names out of her. Leading the charge against Georgia was one particular girl who'd been friends with her for ages, right from when they were littlies at nursery. Sometime between then and now, a switch had flipped in her head and she'd decided to turn on her.

Once again, I suggested Georgia think about a new start somewhere else. Instead, she had a different idea. She was turning nine, and with the big day approaching, we began arranging her birthday party.

"Who do you want to invite this year?" I asked her.

Georgia counted out a list of names on her fingers – but my jaw dropped when she included the name of the chief bully who'd been making her life hell for years.

"Are you sure?" I said. The thought of this kid in our home, singing happy birthday as Georgia blew out the candles on her cake, made my stomach turn. "She's been so nasty to you."

But Georgia blinked back at me and said: "I thought that if I could just show her we can be friends, it might put an end to it."

I swallowed hard against the lump in my throat. That moment just sums up the kind of kid she was, how thoughtful. We did as Georgia wanted, even taking this girl on a day out with Georgia to Cadbury World, thinking it would be a good chance for them to bond. They laughed and squealed together, dizzy on chocolate highs. For the most part you'd never know to look at this girl what she was capable of. But every now and then, the facade would slip. *I see you, madam*, I thought. *I see you.*

When Georgia's plan failed to deliver, we reluctantly got the school involved.

"They haven't taken a blind bit of notice," I told Steve, as I cleaned up Georgia's latest scrape. "What do we have to do?"

"Right," said Steve, grabbing his coat. "Enough's enough."

"Where are you going?"

"To see the head."

At the school, Steve literally laid down the law. "This has got to stop – and you're going to do something about it," he said.

"Pretty soon these kids will be ten years of age. Perhaps you're not aware, but that's the age of criminal responsibility. If you don't start enforcing some rules, as soon as they're ten I'm getting the police involved."

It seemed to spur them into action. From that day forward, the school rang me every afternoon, letting me know how Georgia had got on and telling me if there'd been any incidents. With Georgia's reluctant help, all the bullies were identified and the ringleader's parents were summoned to the head for a talking to.

For a while, things did calm down, but this one girl was sly and persistent. Now and then, she succeeded in rallying the other kids to rough Georgia up. They tripped her over, barged into her and shoved her off playground furniture. My heart ached for her, I just wanted her to feel safe, happy and secure. I couldn't get my head around how being a polite, pretty child with a gentle manner about you could mark you out as a target for bullies. It was as though she was *too* nice for them. And it wasn't in Georgia's nature to fight back, instead she just seemed to soak up the blows.

As the primary school years came to an end, I breathed a sigh of relief. Sure enough, Georgia followed her sister to Ercall Wood. The bullies who'd caused her so much hurt vanished from her life for good.

After years under their thumb, bullied into submission, Georgia had a new-found, boundless energy. There was running, tennis, and clubs after school. She did canoeing and climbing on trips to the outdoor education centre in North Wales, and canyoning in icy cold mountain streams. She was passionate about her role as a mentor to other pupils, because it meant looking out for kids who were being bullied, and she knew all too well what the warning signs were. Georgia would have a go at anything. She was a live wire, constantly on the go.

One day, she piled in from school and I asked her what she wanted for tea.

"Can I have a fish pie out the freezer?"

Fish pie was her go-to when she was in a hurry. A quick 20 minutes in the oven and they were done.

"Where are you running off to now?" I asked.

"I'm going back to school. There's an open night, and I put my name down to guide the parents."

"Really?" I said. "Why don't you just calm down and have a break?"

"No, I promised them, Mum!" she said.

Sometimes my head span just trying to keep up with Georgia. We needed a way of channelling her enthusiasm, something recreational that would soak up some of that energy and teach her a few new skills at the same time.

"One of the lads at work is a supervisor at the Air Cadets in Wellington," Steve said. "I'll ask him if any other girls go."

He told Steve to bring Georgia down for a taster night, so we went together to introduce her. The cadets were based in a squat, two storey building with a square of tarmac to the side where they practised marching. Georgia's face lit up as soon as we arrived. Steve and I were only there ten minutes – she slotted straight in.

"How did you get on then?" I asked her later.

The words tumbled out of Georgia in a breathless torrent. "We did drill, I made some new friends, and next week they're doing night exercises in the college over the road!" she thrilled. "Can I come back? If I keep going I can have my uniform in three weeks!"

Those three weeks couldn't pass quickly enough. Georgia got her uniform, and Steve showed her how to iron sharp creases in her shirt by slipping a crisp sheet of brown paper between the folds. He taught her how to polish her cadet boots to a high sheen. Meanwhile I became an expert at knotting Georgia's thick hair into a tight bun, pinning it into place with a hair net so it sat neatly below the leather headband of her beret. There were no half measures with Georgia. She was always immaculately turned out.

Pretty soon, cadets became the mainstay of Georgia's social life. There were weekend camps, sports events at the RAF base in Cosford, flights in gliders and shooting contests.

"I'm a better shot than the boys!" Georgia announced proudly after one competition.

One bonfire night, the cadets were tasked with marshalling the cars for the firework display over at the cricket ground. As our house was the closest, all the kids came to ours to get changed and they walked on from there with Georgia. While they were sorting out their uniforms I heard one of the boys ask Georgia: "Hey Ferret – do you know where my beret is?"

Ferret? I wondered. *What's that all about?*

Later, we found out how she'd earned her nickname. Kids were always forgetting to bring bits of kit when they turned up at camp. Rather than let them suffer a dressing-down from the sergeant, Georgia would go round all the other cadets ferreting out the missing items so they didn't get in bother.

Another weekend, Steve and I picked up Georgia and her school friend, Katy, from Nescliffe Training Camp near Shrewsbury. The ground was flecked with sleet and as we pulled into the car park we caught sight of the pair of them, waiting sodden in the drizzle with their backpacks beside their muddy boots.

"Look at the state of them!" Steve remarked.

They were covered head to toe in muck, hair plastered to their foreheads and mud caked on their cheeks like tribal warriors.

"They look like two drowned rats! God – I hope they enjoyed it!" I said.

Shivering, teeth chattering against the cold, the girls threw their packs into the boot, and climbed into the back of the car. All the way home, we couldn't shut them up.

"We went on night manoeuvres! We found a concrete bunker and slept inside, but it was so cold we had to light a fire just to keep warm! It was brilliant!"

Katy had the same mad sense of humour as Georgia. They recounted their stories of their weekend with so much enthusiasm we felt like we'd shivered through it with them, and spent the night huddling around their little campfire. That's the kind of camaraderie they enjoyed in cadets. No one was trying to be Mr or Mrs Big. They were all lovely kids who looked out for each other. Maybe it was this warmth – rather than the campfires – that Georgia was drawn to.

One day, Georgia came home from school bursting with excitement. "The school's building a plane!" she said. "There's an open evening for parents – will you come?"

Steve and I looked at each other as if to say, *all this fuss over putting a little model together.* But Georgia was buzzing about it so we thought we'd better humour her.

"Yes, we'll be there," Steve said, rolling his eyes.

When the evening came, we followed Georgia to the design and technology department. She could hardly contain herself. Inside were large crates full of aeroplane parts, packs of nuts and bolts and a shiny new engine sat on a pallet covered in shrink wrap.

I nudged Steve. "I think we've got our wires crossed here."

"I'm thinking the same," he said, surveying the mass of parts laid out on the floor.

"Georgia?" I said. "When you told us they were building a plane, did you mean an *actual* plane?"

"What did you think I meant?" she said.

It turned out the school was one of several around the country who'd applied for this build-a-plane scheme, sponsored by Boeing. Ercall Wood had been chosen to receive the first one. A whole plane for free! All the kids had to do now was put it together – like an Airfix kit, but on a massive scale. The teachers were looking for students to go along and help build the kit, and obviously Georgia's hand had shot up first. They drafted in retired aircraft technicians and pilots from RAF Cosford to help decipher the plans and put the parts together. It was another after school activity for Georgia and – because she was so slim and petite – she was a real asset.

"She gets her hands into all the little nooks and crannies," her teacher told me.

The plane was going to take years to build. Alongside the practical work, Georgia went to meet the directors at Boeing. She gave a talk in the Houses of Parliament about girls working in science and technology, showing MPs how girls were just as capable as boys at technical jobs.

Cadets, and now this plane project, had ignited something in Georgia. Her fascination with military life was more than an evening and weekend diversion. The way she took such pride over her uniform, her determination to prove she could be as good – or even better – than the boys. She'd found her niche. Georgia was quite literally aiming for the skies.

As the girls grew up, the house was always full of light and laughter. Their friends were like extended family. Tabitha and Katy would stop over at weekends. When Jadine, still in her teens, became a mum herself, we took her daughter with us on days out and trips to the theatre. Georgia gathered mates from all over the place on her cadet camps, and every now and then they'd descend on ours for camping trips up the Wrekin or the Ercall. Sunday mornings would be a flurry of activity as they came down from the hill to use the loo and freshen up. They'd stock up on provisions and be off again.

I thought that between us, Steve and I had done a good job with our girls. Now Scarlett and Georgia were more independent, I was keen to give some less fortunate kids the same, sure footing on the future, and the experience of life in a stable, loving family. I'd been mulling over the idea of fostering for a while. I'd grown up in a house full of foster kids. Mum had about ten of us to look after at one point. Sometimes it felt like one, long Famous Five adventure.

By this time, Georgia was taking her options, while Scarlett was finishing up at college and sussing out which university she was going to. We had a family conference and broached it with them.

"We've been talking about fostering," I said. "What do you think?"

They were all for it. My mum and dad still fostered so the girls had grown up with my sprawling family.

"Your lot turned out alright!" said Scarlett.

Georgia was really excited. We had the garage converted into an extra bedroom, and Scarlett moved in there so she could creep home without disturbing us when she'd been out clubbing. We embarked on months of training and assessments to become approved foster carers.

At one point, an assessor came round the house to interview us. I answered the door to him and had to take a step back as the smell of booze hit me. He reeked of whisky! He toddled in, his big, red nose leading the way like a glowing beacon, and flopped heavily onto the sofa, breathing fumes. Then he proceeded to interview Steve and me, scribbling notes on his pad, somehow without even looking at it. It's a wonder he could even focus.

"And I'll need to take the name and address of a referee," he slurred.

Steve lined up Phil Pledger, one of the inspectors at work, and told him this assessor would be in touch for a face-to-face interview. Weeks passed. The chap cancelled the first appointment and – on the second one – he turned up hours late and so drunk he didn't even make it into the house.

"He was pissed again!" Steve told me when he came home from work one evening. "Phil chucked him off the doorstep!"

The next time he came to ours he was on his best behaviour – sober and sheepish. He sat down and said: "Do you think you could provide me with an alternative reference? On reflection, we don't think such a close work colleague is the best option."

I had to stifle a laugh because of course we knew the truth of what had gone on.

By the time we finally got the green light, Scarlett was in uni and Georgia had turned 15. We were asked to take on a little two-and-a-half-year-old boy, David. He had his own room upstairs, and we put a gate across the stairs to stop him falling down if he came toddling out on his own. The first night, I put him to bed and later, when we were turning in ourselves, I popped my head around the door to check on him.

My heart froze. David's bed was empty.

"Steve!" I yelled. "Steve – he's gone!"

I was pulling my hair out. Our first foster child – and I'd gone and blimmin' lost him! Steve, Georgia and me tore round the house looking for David.

"It doesn't make sense! The stair gate was on the whole time!" I said.

"There's no way he could have opened that," Steve replied. "Let's just backtrack a minute."

Steve went back to David's bedroom and had a proper look around. "Lynnette!" he called. "Come and look at this."

Relief washed over me. There, curled on the floor at the foot of his bed, was little David. Somehow he'd slipped off the end in his sleep, and I'd completely missed him when I'd put my head around the door. After that, some nights I took to lying on the floor next to David's bed, holding his tiny hand in mine until he dropped off to sleep.

He was only with us a couple of weeks before a 14-year-old girl, Lucy, came to stay with us. We'd told the council from the outset that we were willing to take on difficult children. Scarlett had had a few 'Kevin the teenager' moments growing up but, for the most part, our two had been good as gold. Our experience of 'difficult' amounted to a bit of moodiness, perhaps the odd slammed door if things got really bad.

The first day we met her, Lucy came wobbling into the house on three-inch heels, wearing eyeliner, false lashes and a skirt like a belt. Steve clapped a hand over his forehead as if to say, *here we go! What have we let ourselves in for?!*

The social worker introduced us and we gathered in the front room to talk about how we liked to do things together as a family. We began explaining how mealtimes worked and I said: "We always like to sit at the table and have a proper meal together. Steve usually does a big breakfast on Sunday mornings…"

The social worker raised a palm and brought me to an abrupt halt. "Lucy doesn't have tea with her foster parents," she said. "She'll be given five pounds a night, and she can go and buy her own in McDonald's."

"Hmm," I said. "Well – no. That's not really how we do things here. We'd prefer it if she had tea with us."

Lucy looked aghast, her bright red lips twisted into an angry pout.

"The thing is, she usually goes out to see her friends after that," the social worker chipped in.

"OK, where does she go?" Steve asked.

"I'm not telling you," Lucy said.

"We've got to know where you are," said Steve. "For your own safety. We always know where our two are."

"Lucy can just call you when she wants picking up," the social worker told Steve. "Usually between ten and half past."

Steve nearly choked on his tea. "Ten and half past? On a school night? I'm sorry, but we're not doing that. It's not happening."

The first few days, I'd pick Lucy up from school and as soon as she was out of the gates, her phone rang hot. She cupped her hand over her mouth and spoke in half whispers. In reply, I caught snatches of male voices on the other end. Men's voices – not boys'.

It got to the first Friday and Lucy was due her pocket money. Steve handed over the cash, and Lucy asked: "Can I go to a party tonight?"

"Yeah, OK. What time until?" Steve said.

Lucy slumped. "No – it's all night."

"You can't really stay out all night. Where is it you're going?"

"I'm not telling you!" Lucy said, crossing her arms in defiance.

"Look, if we drive you there, speak to the parents and make sure it's OK with them…"

"Oh just forget it!" Lucy snapped. "Can I at least go to the garage for some sweets?"

Georgia had been watching in disbelief from the sidelines. "I'll go with her," she said.

The garage was only a hundred yards round the corner. I didn't think anything could possibly go wrong, but Steve took Georgia to one side before they left.

"See how you get on, but if anything happens – don't get involved," he said.

Off they went together. They were only gone a few minutes when Georgia came bounding back in the house, breathless.

"She's run away!" Georgia said. "I did as you said, Dad. I didn't try to stop her!"

"Yeah – you did the right thing," Steve said.

The next few hours were a taste of what was to come for us as a family. Hours of anxious waiting. Police scouring the house, searching every corner from the loft to the garden. Pacing and tea drinking through a long, sleepless night.

But eight o'clock the next morning, Lucy turned up on the doorstep, eyes like saucers, high as a kite.

"I haven't done anything!" Lucy complained.

"I think you're forgetting what I do for a living – I know what people look like when they've taken drugs – and you're the very picture!" Steve said.

"Can I just go to bed? I've been up all night." Lucy huffed.

I waved her upstairs. "Go on. Get some sleep."

Georgia was always level-headed in times like this, when fostering upset the usual rhythm of routine in the house. Later, when Georgia was about 16, we were caring for another girl, Maxine. She was easier-going than Lucy and even went to cadets with Georgia for a while. But she still had her moments. There was a time one winter when the ground was covered in a thick layer of snow, so deep the school announced it had to close. Maxine couldn't get her head around it and spiralled into a tantrum about being stopped from doing what she wanted.

"No one's *stopping* us from going," Georgia counselled. "It's closed. Look – there's no cars on the road. The snow's too deep."

Maxine saw sense and the mood suddenly lifted like sunshine after a spring thunderstorm. I gave Georgia a little nod. *Thank you – well done.*

In the meantime, Steve's police career had gone from strength to strength. By the time Georgia was 12, he'd moved from CID to the police intelligence unit, picking up a load of commendations for outstanding police work along the way. One evening he came home from work.

"Good day, love?" I asked him.

"Yes, it was a good day…" he said distractedly, trailing off.

"What do you fancy for tea?"

Steve stared into nothingness, lost in thought.

"Steve?"

He came to his senses and said: "I think I've got him."

"Got who?"

"That kidnap – 15 months ago, remember? I think I've got him."

"You're joking?"

I remembered it well. It was the kind of horrific crime you struggled to forget. A man had pounced on a couple parked up in a car and asked for a lift. When they refused, he kidnapped them both, then kicked the guy out and forced the woman to drive to a deserted lane where he'd raped her. It had ruined her life, cost her her job – everything. West Mercia Police declared the crime a major incident and threw 30 officers – Steve among them – at the job. There'd been some dissent among the ranks because some officers thought it was too bizarre to be credible, but Steve insisted it was taken seriously, and for three exhausting months it became all consuming. The girls and I said our goodnights long before Steve came home from work, and he'd be gone before we woke the next morning. They left no stone unturned but – frustratingly – at the end of it all, they drew a blank. I knew that failing to crack the case plagued Steve. Any good detective struggles to let go, but the plight of these two victims was a source of torment. He'd been driven to find this guy because he didn't want him ruining anyone else's life – and the hard work had come to nothing.

Only now – over a year later – he'd had a breakthrough.

A job had come in a few days ago. A guy had approached a man and two women in a car outside a club in Wellington. Like before, he'd kidnapped them. This time he'd robbed everyone and sexually assaulted one of the women. A photo of a potential suspect had appeared in the *Shropshire Star* and a member of the public had called in with a name.

The new case clearly rang alarm bells for Steve.

"It's got to be the same guy," he said. "I'm sure of it. There's just too many similarities."

Steve had run the name – Neil Garmson – past some colleagues who dealt with sexual offenders. Sure enough, they had a file on him. Over a decade before, while serving in the army as a chef, he'd indecently assaulted four women. Only it hadn't flagged up on the main computer a year ago when Steve and his colleagues had been searching for known sex offenders.

"It doesn't seem right," Steve said, shaking his head. "Something to do with him being dealt with at an army court martial rather than as a civilian. If only we'd known!"

To Steve, it was all adding up. He went through the two incidents with a fine-tooth comb, detailing all the parallels between the cases. He was adamant he had his man. But there was still a long way to go.

"I've got it past the inspector," he told me proudly one day.

"What did he say?"

"I was just in time. He was about to file it away for good. He said if I'm right and we get a conviction, he'll buy me a bottle of scotch."

Well then, Steve will be having a bottle of scotch, I thought to myself.

Over the next six months, Steve built his case against Garmson. Finally, he had his moment in court. After a ten-day trial, Garmson was convicted of two rapes, three robberies and two sexual assaults, as well as five counts of kidnap. Steve was ecstatic.

"Where's that bottle of whisky, then?" I asked when he returned home empty-handed.

"Mmh. About that – the boss stood up and took all the credit in court. He did apologise and I told him I wasn't bothered, but I said he could stick his whisky up his arse!"

It was a lighter moment in what had been an emotional day. After the verdict, outside the court, the victim had run up to Steve to thank him.

"You know what she said?" Steve began. "She told me – never mind what went on in court, she knows the case would never have been solved if I hadn't stuck with it. She said I've given her her life back."

I couldn't comprehend what this woman had been through, but knowing Steve had somehow helped her move on made the girls and I glow with pride. He always tried to do right by the victims. There were times Steve got flak for being a policeman, or I'd overhear someone slagging off the police force. I always stepped in and stuck up for them, because I assumed every officer was like Steve, putting in 110%. That's why when everything happened to us, it felt like such a betrayal. I suddenly realised not every police officer was as hard working or as committed as Steve.

And that commitment didn't go unnoticed. Not long after Garmson was locked away, Steve moved up to West Mercia's Major Investigation Unit, or MIU, the specialist team which investigated the region's most serious crimes – offences like murder, kidnap and stranger rape. Then, in November 2009, all four of us got dolled up for an evening at the Madeley Court Hotel in Telford. Steve and the other two officers who'd got Neil Garmson locked up for nine years were awarded the Chief Constable's Commendation – the highest honour the force can bestow on a serving officer. After Steve took to the stage, the girls and I lined up alongside him, trying not to blink against the white flash of a photographer's camera. Georgia – 14 years old and dressed in a smart black shirt – proudly tucked a hand in the crook of her dad's elbow, and rested a palm over his forearm. Her auburn hair shone. She looked every inch the proud daughter.

Georgia sailed through those last couple of years at school, first as a prefect and finally as head girl. The plane she'd started building almost five years earlier still wasn't quite finished by the time she left, but after enrolling at New College, she vowed to return and put those slender hands to work on the plane's awkward nooks and crannies.

One evening, Georgia walked in from the local garage looking a little flushed. "That lad from the garage has just asked me out!" she told Steve.

"What did he say?" he asked.

"He asked for my telephone number."

"What did you do?"

"I made one up!" Georgia shrugged.

This was a little trick she'd learned from Scarlett. "If you don't like the lad, just give him the wrong telephone number," she'd told her.

We didn't make a big deal of it. It was just another sign that our little girl was no longer so little. She was growing up, spreading her wings. A-level college meant new friends, new freedoms and new experiences. A lot of the kids had started going to the local pub, the Haygate, where the hopeful young indie bands from the local college strummed and clattered out their teenage angst. At first, when Georgia asked if she could go, Steve said a firm 'no', because he thought she was still a little young. But he did a bit of research on the quiet and discovered the pub had an annex which was a real teen hangout on gig nights. Parents would go down and watch the kids playing, and the staff had a strict policy on underage drinking. Not only that, but it was actually a favourite watering hole among quite a few police officers.

"All right Georgia," we told her innocently. "We've had a think about it and decided you can go."

We had to laugh when she found out why.

"Now I know why you said I could go – it's full of Dad's mates! You've got eyes on me!" she said with mock indignation.

Some evenings, we'd walk in the house and the latest Haygate band would be sprawled on the sofa, buzzing from the energy of the gig, because Georgia knew them all from college, and she'd brought them back to ours. There were some weird-looking lads among them, but they were always decent kids.

Another night, Georgia and a couple of her girlfriends were getting ready to go out.

"Where are you off to then?" I asked.

"Cinema," Georgia replied. "We're just waiting for Jamie from up the road to pick us up."

"Jamie?"

"You know Jamie – from the garage."

I pictured the meek-looking boy behind the counter at the petrol station, quietly swiping Nectar cards and ringing up snacks, and realised it must have been the same boy who'd asked for her number weeks earlier.

"Oh – that's Jamie!" I said. "Well – have a good time and make sure he doesn't bring you home too late."

After that, Jamie showed up at the house more and more frequently. He never came in the house, never even came to the door. He'd just sit at the top of the drive in the car, picking up and dropping off. It was always Georgia and at least a couple of friends – Jamie never once picked her up alone. Steve even went out to him one evening.

"They're just getting their coats – you can come in if you want," he told him.

"It's OK, I'll just wait here if they're on the way," Jamie replied.

Steve wasn't shy, and as Georgia and her mates got ready one evening, he asked one of them: "Is Jamie your boyfriend?"

"No!" she scoffed. "He's just a friend."

None of us saw him as a threat, even when Scarlett twigged who he was and piped up: "Jamie Reynolds! I went to school with him."

It meant there was a five-year age gap between him and Georgia, but by the time we realised, he'd picked the girls up so often that I'd grown used to the idea of them all hanging out together. And who was I to talk? I was only 16 and Steve was the 21-year-old boy next door when we got together.

Jamie was just one of the gang. He was on the fringes – because we heard other boys' names bandied around far more regularly – and with more excitement – than his, but he was one of the gang nonetheless. The girls all saw him as harmless. So harmless that if it got to the end of the night and Jamie was left heading home alone, one of them would walk back through the park with him, just to make sure he got there in one piece. They thought if anyone was going to get beaten up walking home alone in the dark, it would be him.

Georgia's feelings for Jamie were purely platonic. A couple of times I asked her straight: "Is he your boyfriend?"

Her reply was always the same. "Oh my God! No!"

But whatever her intentions towards him, Jamie felt differently about her. One evening she got home from the Haygate and plopped on to the sofa. Perhaps I could tell there was something preying on her mind, because I asked: "Did you have a good night? Anything exciting happen?"

"I did have a bit of a surprise," Georgia said, cupping her cheeks in her hands. "Jamie asked me out."

"Oh right," I said. "And how do you feel about that?"

"He's more of a mate than anything, Mum," she said. "I told him I don't want to ruin our friendship."

That was it. We never heard any more. She'd handled it well, in the way she wanted. She'd turned him down sensitively, and she was determined to move forward past any lingering awkwardness.

Not long after that, Georgia came home one day and told us she'd met a boy – he'd chatted her up on the bus of all places.

"He's called Matt," she said. "Matt Bird."

She'd been sat in the middle of the top deck, and a lad behind her started winding her up and generally being a pest. Matt was sat at the back but saw what was going on, so he moved up to sit next to Georgia and started chatting to her as though he was a mate. He diffused the whole situation.

"I've never had that as a pickup line before," she laughed. "But I don't mind because he's really nice!"

"I suppose he got the right phone number then?!" I said.

Georgia's smile said it all.

We started seeing a fair bit of Matt after that. He'd pick her up to take her out. Georgia would watch him play rugby. I remember her being bowled over when a bouquet arrived at the house. She ran to Steve, thrilled, and said: "Dad! He's sent me flowers! The first flowers I've ever had off a boy!"

They were a good match, and they would have made a lovely little couple. Matt was the sort of lad you hope your daughter will bring home – polite, kind and confident. And – like Georgia – he knew what he wanted in life.

I'd suspected years before when Georgia joined the air cadets that it was really the first step of an RAF career for her. Now at college, she'd tailored her A-levels with an eye on joining up – and she was determined to get as close as possible to the action. At that time, women weren't allowed to actually fight, so Georgia's plan was to become a field paramedic. I was worried, to be honest. She had a dream, and I wasn't for a minute going to put her off it, but I did try and steer her away from the front line.

"I mean – there's other things you can do in the RAF," I said. "Have you thought about working in one of the support crews?"

But she was adamant. "No, this is what I want to do," she said. She couldn't go in with a gun – even though she was a better shot than the boys – so paramedic it was.

Georgia knew she needed academic subjects, so she'd signed up for biology and psychology A-levels. But her real zeal was for outdoor education. In March 2013, I took her to the RAF recruitment office in Shrewsbury to discuss her next steps, and to find out if she was taking the right subjects for whatever roles she might want to pursue.

I think I felt more nervous than Georgia as we arrived. The staff walked out from the back office dressed smartly in uniform, and I was trying to be formal and proper as I began introducing us.

"Oh, hello Georgia!" they said, relaxed and casual – like they were propping up a bar. "Good to see you! How you getting on? Come on through."

We followed the sergeant through to his office. "Don't tell me you're thinking of joining up?" he teased.

Georgia nodded eagerly, then laid out her plans to become a field paramedic.

"We'd be very happy to have you," he said, before explaining her options. She could join up straight after college and get trained on the job, or they'd fund her through university, studying for a paramedic qualification, as long as she committed to a minimum term of service in the RAF when she finished.

Scarlett had loved university life, her third year studying history had taken her overseas to Arizona, and I'd often catch Georgia laughing as her sister regaled her with the latest on uni over Skype. I reckon Georgia was weighing it all up and possibly thinking, *sounds like the life for me.* The flip side was, if she joined up, she could start earning straight away. Georgia came away chuffed, on a high. She'd been apprehensive that taking outdoor education might have scuppered her chances of making it into the RAF as a paramedic, but the psychology and biology suited her ambitions to a tee. To my mind, and Steve's, she was leaning towards joining straight from college.

Georgia's future was taking shape. She had it all mapped out.

Barely two months later, it was all taken away.

FOUR

I've replayed that weekend of May 2013 over and over so many times. Even now – through the long, sleepless nights, or in the still of morning before everyone stirs – it's often all I can think about. But no matter what angle I look at it from, there's not even the tiniest hint of what was to come. Of how our lives would be reduced to just a hollow existence. Of how every shared and private moment would be stripped of joy. Of how simple pleasures like a meal out, or a trip abroad, would become nothing more than a bit of temporary relief from our heartbreak.

It began with a Saturday identical to umpteen others over the last ten years. My dad had been a keen football ref back in the day. After a heart attack in his fifties, he'd hung up his boots for good, but he still loved the sport and wasn't ready to give up on it entirely. So he'd turned to fundraising for AFC Telford United – and Georgia was his secret weapon. She'd been helping him hawk his match day tombola tickets up and down the raucous terraces since she was about seven years old. Together, they'd raised thousands of pounds for the club. Sometimes, in the heat of a controversial decision or missed goal, the screaming fans would turn the air blue with their swearing. But when they saw our Georgia nudging her way through the crowds, her big brown eyes shining, even the most foul-mouthed supporters were on their absolute best behaviour.

"You know what they all say?" Dad told me. "'I won't buy a ticket from you, John. I'll have one off the littlun. She'll bring me luck!'"

I dropped Georgia off at the ground just after lunch, knowing Dad would be in the back somewhere to meet her. Of course, now – at 17 years old – she wasn't so little anymore, and she'd been promoted from helping Dad sell his tickets. Instead, she was up in the stadium offices with the little team of volunteer accountants. Her job was to keep the hungry turnstiles fed with bags of change. Then, while the players slogged it out on the pitch, she totted up the takings from the gates.

Driving home, I mentally ticked off the long list of things that made up Georgia's busy half term week ahead. It was – as usual – non-stop. Shopping in Telford, a big gig in Wolverhampton with her mates, her first driving lesson, a couple of days out with Matt.

And those blimmin' photos for Jamie, I tutted, shaking my head.

By now, Jamie had moved on from the garage for a job in the Savers shop. But he absolutely loathed it, and Georgia had filled me in on his big plans to become a photographer. First off, he needed to get a portfolio together to show everyone what he could do.

"He's asked me to model for him," Georgia had revealed.

She'd told him loads of times she wasn't interested, but her friends had agreed to take part, so Georgia did, too. Plus, Jamie was a mate who needed help, and Georgia believed passionately that mates look out for one another. But I was far from convinced. I didn't want her taken advantage of, and this sounded like a recipe for certain trouble.

"I'm not sure I'm happy about it," I responded disapprovingly. I didn't think for a second that she might be in any danger, but I was imagining topless pictures, or – worse – nudity. "What sort of photos are we on about?" I probed. "I don't want anything stupid, and I don't want you doing any photos you'll regret."

"Don't worry It's nothing like *that*," Georgia retorted. "We're meant to be dressing up like biker chicks. There's a few of us going, and Jamie's dad will be there."

"A few? Go on…" I said.

She gave me the names of a couple of good friends. I knew them both. They were girls we trusted and had known for years, friends who'd stayed for Saturday night sleepovers and laughed with us at the kitchen table over Steve's legendary Sunday fry-ups.

I was reassured – as much as any mum can be. "Well, OK. I suppose," I said, and left it at that.

It was late afternoon before Dad dropped her off home from the football. They always stopped at the clubhouse after the game – a pint for him and a coke for Georgia. She came in with a beaming smile, still buzzing from the electric atmosphere of the match.

"How did you get on today?" I said.

"Oh, you know – just been hanging out with the players after the game," she grinned.

It was only a small club, and they weren't big-name players, but Georgia loved it all the same. Whatever she was doing, she always did it joyfully.

Later that night, Georgia, Maxine, Steve and I relaxed in front of Saturday night TV with a takeaway curry and bars of chocolate for afters. We all had our favourites. Georgia always went for Toffee Crisp or Bueno, Maxine had a thing for chocolate with Smarties in it, while Steve was your more traditional fruit and nut type. We were swapping and sharing, all having a bit of each other's. It sounds silly, remembering a little thing like that, but you don't realise how special those ordinary nights on the sofa are until they're gone forever.

The next day, Sunday May 26th 2013, I was taking Georgia shopping in town. Visitors to Telford remember it for its roundabouts, concrete and bypasses, but one thing we do really well is shopping centres! Steve was working a case, otherwise he'd have come with us, and I don't mean just to keep us company. Those bored-looking men you see stood outside Top Shop waiting for their wives, girlfriends or daughters? That's not Steve – he actually loves shopping! He's usually the one grabbing hangers off the rail and saying: "Go on, try this on. This might be nice!"

We always took the mickey out of him. "He's looking for himself, really!" we'd tease. "He just wants us to buy stuff so he can spend on himself without feeling guilty!"

But, as I say, that weekend, Steve's unit had a job on, and it was all hands on deck until they caught whoever they were looking for. Meanwhile Georgia was due away on a college outdoor education trip in three weeks' time. Canoeing, rock climbing and trekking in the Loire Valley and the Dordogne – it was right up her street. She'd marched her tired, old walking boots half to death, and we'd already replaced them with a new pair. Now I wanted to buy her some nice little bits for their stop in Paris on the way back.

"How about these?" I said, picking out a pair of floaty culottes in orange and blue, her favourite colours.

Georgia nodded enthusiastically. "Let me try them on!" she said, and disappeared off into the changing room.

She was just starting to show a proper interest in clothes and fashion. Until then, she'd been more of a practical, jeans and jumpers, type of girl, because she was so into cadets, and outdoor sports. But now, she'd grown her hair long, gained a few inches in height and had begun – under Scarlett's careful supervision – experimenting with a bit of make-up. There'd been times when I'd caught her moaning about the shape of her body. "Look at me! I'm straight up and down. No waist!" she'd complain. But

Scarlett had been selling a few vintage dresses on eBay to help pay her way through uni, and she'd asked Georgia to wear them for some photos. When she twirled in front of the mirror and posed for Scarlett's camera, you could see the realisation dawning: *I've got a few curves now. I'm not so bad after all!*

Now, she came out of the cubicle to show me the culottes.

"What do you think?" she said.

I gave her the thumbs up. They suited her to a tee. Georgia was going to take Paris by storm!

"Perfect," I said. "But we're not done yet!"

We headed on to Zara – we were both big fans. Georgia had discovered the chain a few years back on one of our trips to Spain, before it got really well known over here. She was drawn to how different the clothes looked compared to the trends back home, and she loved that she could buy gear that none of her friends would have.

"They'll all want to know where I got them from," she'd grin, mischievously. "I'll just tell them – *Spain!*"

We hunted down a royal blue blazer to pair the culottes with, then found a couple of tops, and some new trekking shorts. After a bite to eat and a latte it was on to Primark to meet a pal of Georgia's, who had a spare ticket for the gig the next day: *Slamdunk.* It was a one-day festival with loads of bands playing over several stages. Georgia and her friends had been planning their big day out for weeks. I'd made sure I knew all the details – who was going, travel arrangements, how they were getting there and back.

Georgia was meeting Matt and some friends at the station, they were travelling over to Wolverhampton as a group, and then coming back together after the gig. A few others were going, too, and Georgia was meeting them in the venue.

I had no concerns. Georgia was already going down the Haygate, and she'd proved we could trust her. She wasn't the sort to go out and get steaming drunk. She always made it home on time, and if I set limits on her socialising, she always accepted them, without any of the backchat you expect from teenagers.

Georgia and I arrived home loaded down with bags of shopping to find an early summer sun bathing the garden in a warm glow. It was ideal barbecue weather, and after a bit of umming and ahhing we decided to fire it up. Scarlett had finished uni by now, and she'd started her first job, as an auctioneer's assistant in the jewellery quarter up in Birmingham. With no studies or exams to worry about, she came over, and together we had a stab at getting the barbecue going. In the meantime, Georgia was preoccupied with giving her hair a fresh tint.

"What do you think, Mum?" she said, holding a bunch of locks to the light. "Shall I do it now or in the week?"

Her striking, auburn red colour had started to fade, and it needed brightening up. I'd bought her a new pack of dye.

"You're so busy next week – how are you going to find time to fit that in?" I said.

"Good point – I'll do it now."

She left Scarlett and I to tinker with the barbecue, and it wasn't long before my mum and dad joined us, before Steve arrived home from work about 5pm. As men do, he started organising the barbecue duties straight away. He'd worked seven long days straight and had run around the depths of Shropshire to pin down all his necessary enquiries. Now, with the week ahead booked off on annual leave, he could relax.

While Steve was in the kitchen prepping the food, Georgia – her locks now restored to their glowing beauty – was sorting out some clothes for Jamie's photo shoot.

As she smoothed out the creases on her T-shirt with a hissing iron, she asked: "Dad, have you got time to take me out on a driving lesson?"

But Steve was up to his elbows in salad and sausages. "I haven't, mate," he said. "I've got to sort the food out for the barbecue. I can't just leave everyone waiting."

Then, seeing the look of disappointment on Georgia's face, he added: "I tell you what – I'll take you out tomorrow, I've got the week off now."

But Georgia shook her head and explained about the gig in Wolverhampton. She'd be out all day, and it'd be the early hours of the morning before she arrived back home.

"It's OK – we'll have plenty of time in the week," Steve reassured her.

"It's just that I'm feeling a bit worried about this first proper lesson on Tuesday," she said.

She'd already been out in the car with Steve a few times. It was going really well – and Steve told her as much.

"I feel like I'm going to crash and burn!" Georgia sighed, her forehead creasing with a worried frown.

Now Steve put a concerned arm around her. "Don't say things like that," he soothed.

"I don't mean literally, I'm just worried," she replied.

"There's nothing to worry about – millions of people take lessons, and your first one will be very basic. You'll be OK!" Steve said matter-of-factly. He paused a moment, then added: "Are you sure that's what's worrying you?"

"I think so, yeah," Georgia told him.

"Well – you'll be fine," said Steve.

She nodded and gave him a squeeze. "Thanks, Dad," she said, before grabbing her T-shirt and heading off to her room.

It was rare for Georgia to be so fazed by taking on something new. She usually launched herself at fresh challenges with such courage that you were left reeling. But this time, for some reason, her nerves seemed to have bubbled to the surface.

Taking advantage of the warm evening, we all ate together outside in the garden, and any lingering concerns about the driving lesson were forgotten as Dad had everyone laughing at his daft jokes. Scarlett gave us the nitty gritty on the new job, while Steve was kept on his toes making sure everyone had enough to eat. Meanwhile Georgia told us about her plans for the week. Matt's mum had put him on her car insurance, so he and Georgia could make a couple of day trips.

"Do you know where you're going yet?" I asked.

"Mmh, not sure," Georgia replied. "We've been looking at some National Trust places. Maybe the beach if the weather's good."

She had a day's work at the garage planned, too. Plus the concert and the driving lesson. She'd left barely enough time to catch her breath.

And tonight, she was doing Jamie's photo shoot.

No wonder she feels ready to burn out, I thought.

"Why don't you just stop in tonight?" I suggested. "Have a rest and leave this photo thing for another day? You don't want to spoil the gig."

Just then, Steve cottoned on to the conversation and came over to join in. Georgia explained her plans.

"You don't want to be doing that, do you?" Steve said. "Who's taking the photos?"

"Jamie," she told Steve, before he grilled her on who was going to be there.

"And how old is he? Steve asked.

"Twenty-two," Georgia said.

"He's a bit old for you, isn't he?"

"There's five years between you and me!" I said to Steve.

"I promised I'd go," Georgia added. "And it's only up the road."

That was Georgia all over. If she made a promise, she kept it. And she always looked after her friends.

"Well what's Jamie like with you?" Steve said.

"You know – he's just a mate, Dad," Georgia told us. "He really likes me – but he's just a friend."

Scarlett let go a sigh. "I do feel bad for him," she said, her voice loaded with pity. "He was always really quiet in school and he didn't exactly have many friends."

Georgia explained how a lot of them in her little group had begun trying to leave Jamie out of get-togethers. She didn't know why – maybe because he was that bit older. But she always made a special effort to include him. She told us how desperate he was to build a proper career – he had a friend who was already doing well in photography and Jamie believed he could make it, too. He wanted this biker chick look for his portfolio so he could target car magazines. And he'd promised that once he started making money, he'd reward the friends who'd helped kick start his career.

It was obvious both the girls felt a bit sorry for him, and when we realised what a lonely time he must have had at school, and how he was left out of things, Steve and I did, too.

We finished up dinner and it was about 7.45pm when Georgia appeared in all her gear for Jamie's photo shoot. Fair play, she really did look like a biker chick. She wore straight, black jeans with black dolly shoes, and pink socks with sweets embroidered on them. Underneath the leather bomber jacket that Steve and I had bought her for Christmas was a white T-shirt with a big, red London bus.

"You do look the part," I said.

"Just like Olivia Newton-John in *Grease*!" Steve nodded.

But then I frowned as I noticed the time. "Are you sure you have to go tonight?" I said.

"I promised him, and I don't want to let him down," she told us. "I won't be late home. I want to be fresh for tomorrow."

I nodded. "Well – if you've promised him. See you in a bit!'

Then for some reason, we all followed her to the front door to say goodbye and wave her off. She had a hundred kisses off us.

"Have fun," I told her. I still didn't really want her to go, but as far as we were all concerned, she was just helping someone out. You had to feel proud of her. I couldn't deny her that. "Remember what I said about these photos!"

We all stood there waving as Georgia went trotting off down the road. The whole family, together, smiling and happy. I hold on to that last moment because, an hour later, it was all taken away from us.

After she'd left, we sat around watching TV with Scarlett. When she turned in for the night, Steve and I stayed up – keeping one eye on the box and the other on the time. 'Not late' with Georgia meant 10pm, maybe half past at the latest. Yet by 10.30pm, there was no sign of her, and I was growing restless.

"I thought she'd be back by now," I said to Steve.

"Me too," he said. "Maybe she's on her way?"

"I hope so," I said, yawning. I hated going to bed without knowing our girls were home safe and sound, but I thought I'd get under the covers with a book while I waited. "I'm going to go up," I said.

Steve joined me in bed, but neither of us could really settle. I'm the type of mum who can't rest until she hears the door latch go. As I lay awake with my book, listening for the clip clop of Georgia's footsteps outside, the grating thunk of her key slotting into the lock, I must have read and re-read the same sentence a dozen times.

"What's going on?" Steve said, exasperated. "What's she playing at?"

She'd never done anything like this before. It was baffling. I couldn't stand it.

"I'm going to call her," I said, reaching for my mobile.

I dialled Georgia's number and listened – getting crosser by the second – as her phone rang and rang.

"No answer," I said, shaking my head before punching out a text: *Georgia it's late now, where are you? Do you need picking up?*

I held the handset, waiting for a reassuring ping and a message from Georgia. Anything to let us know she was safe. Instead, it lay in my palm, cold and ominously silent, like it was daring me to send another text. So I did: *Georgia, you know the rules. Where are you? You're meant to be back by now.*

Still nothing.

"Well – maybe she's finally rebelling," Steve said. "She's nearly 18, and she's always been really good!"

It was so out of character for Georgia, but perhaps Steve had hit the nail on the head. It was a Bank Holiday weekend, then half term. *She's just stretching her wings,* I told myself, even though – deep down – I didn't really believe it.

"I bet she's just bloody gone on to somebody's house, and she's sleeping there now," I tutted.

Then, just as I turned back to my book, my phone bleeped. Steve and I both jumped.

"That'll be her!" said Steve.

Sure enough, it was a message from Georgia, short and not very sweet: *Gone to friends. Will see you in the morning.*

She'd signed off her text with her usual three kisses – *XXX*.

"Gone to friends!" I exclaimed. "Which friends?!" I wanted to know, because even though it was getting late, I was all for ringing them and checking up.

Where have you gone? I texted back. *You said you were coming home, where are you? Who are you with?*

I didn't have to wait long for a reply, but we weren't getting any more out of her tonight.

I can't message any more – my battery's going XXX.

All we had to go on were the couple of curt replies to my texts, apparently from Georgia. We had no reason to disbelieve her. If anything, at that point, I was more cross and hurt than worried. She seemed OK. But what I couldn't fathom was why she was holding out on me. Growing up, Georgia always told the truth. There's only one time I can remember when she let me down, and it was such a little thing. She was about 13 and she'd been going to this community club at the Wrekin College up the road from us. She was desperate to do cadets as well, but it was two nights a week and there was a clash with the club.

"You can't do both, Georgia," I said. "You'll have to choose."

Of course, she picked cadets, and one night I drove her up there, then waited in the car to see her safely inside. When I came back later to pick her up, they said: "Georgia's not here! We haven't seen her."

"Don't worry, I've got an idea where she's got to," I told them.

The club was only round the corner. Sure enough, I found Georgia there.

"I'm really, really sorry, Mum," she said. "I just wanted to come up here."

"You can't wander off without telling anyone where you're going," I scolded.

It was a lesson learned. She never did it again, and as she got older there was nothing we couldn't talk about. We were so close, nothing was taboo. Sex, boyfriends – I'd give Georgia advice on anything she wanted. I was comfortable broaching any topic, no matter how awkward, even though sometimes it would make her curl up with embarrassment.

Yet now, faced with the little matter of telling me who she was with and where she'd gone, she'd suddenly clammed up, grown defiant.

"That's it I suppose," I shrugged. There was nothing more we could do. Rushing round to Jamie's and making a big fuss was pointless – she'd already told us she'd left. "We'll have to catch her tomorrow."

"You wait, madam!" Steve said. "She's going to get a good talking to."

When morning came it was a relief from an anxious, restless night. I hardly slept, but was up at the crack of dawn. While Steve snoozed on, I gently pushed open the door to Georgia's bedroom. I was longing to find her snug under her duvet, a shock of her red hair splayed across the pillow, having somehow crept in during the night without me hearing. I was kidding myself. Her room was still and empty, her fossil collection gathering dust on the shelves, Tigger and Bluey the bear lying undisturbed on the bed.

Downhearted, I nursed a mug of tea and sent Georgia another text asking where she was. I willed my phone to ping with a reply, and my heart leapt when – not too long after – I got one.

I stayed at friends all night, I'll be back later… my phone's dying too. XXX

I still wanted to know where she'd stayed, but when I tried calling her it went straight to voicemail, and when Steve climbed out of bed a couple of hours later he found me anxiously pacing, fretting.

"Heard anything?" he asked.

"Just a text saying she's at a friend's – but now her battery's gone!" I said. "I've tried ringing, but her phone's off. I just wanted to catch her before she heads to the gig, make sure everything's OK. Why doesn't she just let us know where she is?!"

"Let's give it a bit, then call a few of her friends," Steve replied. "Oh – she's in trouble when she gets home!"

That morning, we were taking Scarlett and Maxine for a potter around Ironbridge. Driving over, we tried to bury our concerns and keep things light. As Maxine's foster carers, we had a special duty to her, and didn't think it fair to burden her with all our worries. I thought a bit of fresh air and a change of scenery might help clear my head, somehow provide some answers, and as we strolled along the bank of the River Severn – its muddy waters slipping silently by – I texted a few of Georgia's friends, while Scarlett discreetly made some calls. The answer was always the same: *I haven't seen her. She might be with so and so. We'll probably see her later.*

I even tried Matt, half expecting to hear Georgia right there beside him. Either way, surely she would have checked in with him for any last-minute gig arrangements. Instead, my heart sank.

"I haven't heard from her, Lynnette. Sorry," he said. "I'm sure there's nothing to worry about though. I'll see her at the station in a bit."

"OK. Take care, love," I told him. "Have a good time tonight."

I hung up, at a loss. At this rate, if I didn't catch Georgia before the gig, it would be the early hours of the morning before I'd get to speak to her. And we were running out of people to call.

Then Scarlett piped up: "What about Jamie? I've got his number somewhere."

"Good idea. Ring him!"

I waited on tenterhooks while Scarlett made the call. But I could soon tell from the look on her face and the noises she was making, she was none the wiser. She hung up, shaking her head.

"He says he felt poorly, so Georgia left with some friends. He can't remember who, exactly," she told me.

I sighed heavily, emotions see-sawing from worry to anger and back again, while Steve sent a few texts asking Georgia to get in touch. Like mine, Steve's messages went unanswered.

"I don't think there's any need to fret," Scarlett soothed. "She'll just be with her mates, having fun."

Scarlett had a different perspective on it. She'd been there – having to check in with Mum and Dad because she'd be late home, or to let us know her plans had changed all of a sudden. But the point was, both the girls had always been so good. They knew the consequences if they overstepped the mark. If I told one of them they were grounded for a week, they knew 100% that I'd stick to it. As a result, the times I'd had to dish out punishments were few and far between. We all knew where we stood.

"You're probably right," I nodded, even though secretly I wasn't convinced at all.

We plodded around a few shops, and stopped off in a cafe. The rich aroma of coffee beans hung in the air – but they just made me think of Georgia and her love of a good, creamy latte. While the tables around us buzzed with conversation, my mind was elsewhere. Where I *really* wanted to be was at home, just in case Georgia phoned there, or turned up at the last minute for a quick change of clothes before heading off to meet the others. I stared in silence into my coffee cup, playing over a dozen different scenarios in my head.

It was no good. "I'm sorry, girls," I told them. "Let's get back. Maybe do this another time, eh?"

Steve nodded in agreement. "I bet she'll be there when we pull up!"

Arriving home, I rushed to open the front door and called out: "Georgia!" I was sure she'd appear on the stairs, fresh from the shower, auburn hair wrapped in a bath towel. But instead, deafening silence rolled back at me. The house was still and empty.

Later, Steve had a drive around the neighbourhood, just on the off chance he might spot Georgia. It was a long shot, because she never wandered the streets, but he was desperate for something practical to do. He even popped in the garage where she worked and got her some extra hours she wanted.

"No sign of her though," Steve told me. We were at a loss. "I've messaged her about those extra hours – and I've told her she's in trouble, too."

"Well – she'll probably be on the way to the gig by now," I shrugged. "She's testing us. That's what it is."

Steve nodded. "I bet she's thinking 'I'm nearly 18 now. I don't have to let Mum and Dad know what I'm doing every second of the day. I can do what I like.' We'll see about that! She's going to have a good talking to when she comes through that door!"

We were on edge for the rest of the day, up and down, constantly checking our phones, or sending texts and trying to call people. We spoke to two other girls who Georgia had said were doing Jamie's biker chick shoot with her. Neither had gone in the end. One decided at the last minute she couldn't be bothered, and the other had felt poorly so she'd stayed at home, too.

"I'm even more confused now – who are these 'friends' she's meant to have left Jamie's with?" I said to Steve.

He shook his head, lost for answers, then said: "Well, look at it this way – she's always told the truth. You know what it's like when your phone runs out and no one's got the right charger. She's probably wrapped up in the excitement of the gig now."

The gig didn't finish until midnight. For me, it couldn't come soon enough. Scarlett, meanwhile, was heading back to her place in Wolverhampton. The gig venue was just over the road, and Georgia had mentioned crashing with her sister if it was proving a hassle to get back.

"I'll text you if she turns up at mine," Scarlett said. "Try not to worry."

Easier said than done. As the night wore on, Steve and I tossed 'what ifs' back and forth, trying to make sense of Georgia's worrying silence.

"You'd think she'd just borrow a friend's phone if hers is dead," I tutted.

"But she won't be able to hear a thing if she's in the gig," Steve replied.

It was hopeless. All we could do was wait… and wait.

Eventually, after spending the entire evening whiling the hours away, midnight passed and we tried calling some of Georgia's friends. We got through to a couple of the girls. They hadn't seen Georgia, but they didn't think it was a problem. I almost felt stupid calling them, spreading our worry and spoiling everyone's night. As far as they were concerned, Georgia was probably with another group, or with Matt. It almost made sense. But whatever excuse or plausible explanation we created, doubt crept in, ready to gnaw it to shreds.

"I'm going to have to go to bed," I said eventually. "I'm meant to be in work tomorrow."

"You go up," Steve said. "I'll stay down here. I'm going to have words when she gets home!"

"Wake me if there's any news," I told him.

Who was I kidding? I barely slept at all. Instead I listened out for the door, and for Steve's showdown with Georgia when she eventually landed home. Hearing him ask "Where the hell have you been?! Me and your mum have been worried sick!" would have been music to my ears. Anger and worry would have given way to blessed relief. There'd be apologies from Georgia, and promises never to frighten us like that again. It'd be a harsh lesson, but a few months down the line, maybe we'd be able to laugh about it.

That was the dream, the happy ending. Except it never came. I was in this dreadful, waking nightmare of not knowing, and dawn found me still stuck in the same place.

But it was about to get worse in ways we could never have imagined.

FIVE

I plodded heavily downstairs, my mind foggy from lack of sleep and the strain of trying to solve this impossible puzzle. I'd lain awake through the night – heart pounding in my throat – endlessly rearranging the pieces into different scenarios that put Georgia in a place of safety. Off camping, a jolly with friends, maybe a sleepover. But every time, the picture was just a little bit off. It never quite rang true. There was always a bit missing – the bit where Georgia called us, or sent a text, to let us know where she was. Now, all I had to show for my efforts was the dull, brooding pain lurking behind my eyes.

Steve, too, had been up all night, waiting for his showdown with Georgia. He'd kept watch on the street outside, and as the orange streetlamp glow gave way to the flat, grey light of early morning, Steve reached a huge decision.

"I think it's time we called the police," he said.

For a second, the implication knocked me sideways. I fought to catch my breath, like I'd taken a sudden plunge into something dark and icy cold. Coming from a real-life detective, the idea of 'calling the police' sounded so improbable. Steve was 'the police'. He'd caught killers and solved crimes so complicated you'd tie yourself in knots just thinking about them. But we'd waited long enough. We'd tried reaching out to Georgia's wide circle of friends, we'd called or texted everyone she knew that we could get in touch with – and we were still none the wiser.

I nodded, slumping a little inside. "Yeah, I think it is," I agreed reluctantly.

For Steve, with his background, it was almost a routine thing. Calling the police was just what you did when someone went AWOL. Bringing in the authorities cast the net that bit wider. And nine times out of ten, after all the stress and anguish, there was a happy ending. The 'missing person' turned up with an explanation so obvious it made you groan, oblivious to all the worry they'd caused.

But I had a growing unease at the possibility of a not so happy ending – because we all know they happen. Awful, life will never be the same again endings. Impossible to even contemplate endings. Those endings, the ones that end up on the television news and in the newspapers, begin the same way as the ones that we never even hear about: with that phone call. I couldn't shake the feeling that by dialling those three numbers, we were admitting out loud that something was wrong.

Almost admitting. Because even then, as we steeled ourselves for taking this huge step, we kept up the pretence.

"I mean – we're going to end up looking silly, when she comes home," Steve said. "She'll be in a tent somewhere having a laugh with her mates."

I joined in, playing along with Steve as we tried to make light of this new, ominous development. "We're going to really embarrass her, getting the police involved!"

"I'll give it half an hour, then make the call," Steve said.

"OK. I'd better get dressed," I told him. "I'm going to run my keys into work, then come back here. I can't face it today."

I'd already decided there was no way I could stand in the shop, smiling and talking about the latest perfumes with the customers. Right now, anything other than finding Georgia was just a triviality, a distraction. But I didn't have my boss's number and she couldn't get in until I opened up.

On autopilot, I drove across town and met her at the door. Handing over my keys, I explained how worried we were.

She totally understood, and told me: "Get going! I'll see you when I see you. I hope you hear from her soon."

It was still early – about 9am – by the time I got home. Steve had already made the call, giving the police operator Georgia's details and explaining our concerns. He'd told them who – as far as we knew – she'd last been with, and they'd promised to send an officer round to take some more details. In the meantime, all we could do was wait.

We paced around the house, stressing, before we found ourselves sat together on the little sofa in the bay window of our bedroom. From there, we could see the street outside, and the park over the road. As we scanned up and down the street, fully expecting Georgia to appear any minute, my mind drifted to Steve's suggestion that she'd headed off into the wilds on an impromptu camping trip. It was a nice idea. But as much as I wanted to believe Georgia was snug in a sleeping bag, or raking over the smouldering embers of a campfire to brew a morning cup of tea, it didn't make sense. In an hour or so's time she was due at that first driving lesson. Even if her nerves had got the better of her, she'd have called to cancel and to let us know. And the rest of her week was already mapped out. Every day was accounted for – there just wasn't room to squeeze in a camping trip.

It was about 10.30am when we heard a knock at the door. We opened it to greet a uniformed police officer.

"Mr and Mrs Williams?" she began. "I've just come to get a few more details about your daughter – Georgia, isn't it?"

"That's right, come in," I said nervously.

We sat together in the front room as the WPC filled out a form. She made a note of Georgia's description, names and addresses of friends, the time we'd last seen her and information about what little contact we'd had since she'd left.

"All we've had is a couple of texts," I said.

"And they came from Georgia?" the officer asked.

"Yes, but we still don't know where she is, and that's really out of character. She's usually so good!"

"I understand, Mrs Williams," she said. "Do you have a picture of Georgia that we could borrow?"

The house was covered in photos of the girls growing up. I thought to myself, *I'd better pick a nice one of her, or she'll go mad when she comes back.*

My eyes settled on a big, framed photograph – taken by a professional – of Georgia in her end of school prom dress about a year earlier. It was the most gorgeous gown. Georgia had looked absolutely stunning.

We'd driven over to Cannock for that dress. My mum found the shop one day when she was shopping for a wedding hat.

"They've got the most amazing choice of prom gowns," Mum said. "Maybe we could all go with Georgia one day?"

I was non-committal at first, because at that stage Georgia had never been that bothered about really girly clothes. "Mmh, we'll see," I said. "She's not one for posh dresses."

But all the excitement at school about the upcoming prom must have got to her, because when we suggested it, she was dead keen. And it turned out the shop Mum had found was an absolute gem. It was amazing, with every style and colour of gown you could imagine. Nothing was too much trouble for the staff. We had three or four hours in there, with a break and a bite to eat in their cafe, as Georgia tried on dress after dress. Finally, she set her heart on a strapless gown in aquamarine. The bodice gathered in pleats at the front, with a sprinkling of diamanté detail, and the fishtail skirt was in sheer satin. I gasped when I saw the price tag, but my mum winked and said: "It was made for her – let me go halves with you."

Mum was right. It looked perfect on her, and it was worth every penny. Georgia was so petite that we'd anticipated needing a load of alterations, but it fit her like a glove. She finished the dress off with a silver, V-shaped necklace, matching drop earrings and a tiara, and a few weeks later, Mum surprised her by taking her back to the shop for a professional photo shoot in all her new finery. Then, on the big night, Mum treated her *again* by booking a chauffeur-driven, vintage car to take Georgia and her friend, Kim, to the ball.

I had tears in my eyes as we waved the girls off, and then Steve and I sneaked along to the Hadley Park House Hotel hoping to catch a glimpse of the kids going inside. We watched – from a safe distance so as not to embarrass anyone – as Georgia swept up the steps with her prom 'date', Ryan. There was nothing romantic between them – they were just friends from school. But as Steve and I looked at each other, bursting with pride, it dawned on us that those innocent, carefree school days were behind her. She'd come so far, blossoming into a beautiful young woman. More than that, the prom night was one of those little milestones on her journey to adulthood. Steve and I had got her this far. She was making her own decisions now, shaping her own future. And she was doing it with such an energy and certainty about what she wanted from life, that it just lifted you up and carried you along with her.

Now, back in our front room, the warm memory of that proud moment was shattered by a jolt of sheer panic as I slid the photo from its frame and handed it to the WPC. I realised I was passing the baton over to the police. The hunt for Georgia was literally out of our hands. All of a sudden, *they* were looking for her. Things were escalating by the second, heading somewhere we'd never thought possible.

"Can I just take some more information about where Georgia was going on Sunday night?" the officer asked.

"She went up to see a chap called Jamie Reynolds," Steve explained. "He's just round the corner. She was meant to be meeting some mates there, but it turns out they didn't go."

"You've spoken to them?"

"On the phone," I said. "We've known them all for years."

"But then Jamie's told our other daughter, Scarlett, that Georgia left his place with some friends," Steve added.

She wrote down everything we said, then asked: "You say Jamie lives 'round the corner' – do you know where, exactly?"

"Avondale Road," Steve said. "It's only five minutes' walk away."

Then the officer turned to her radio. "Control? Can I have a check on Avondale Road in Wellington please? The surname is Reynolds."

We waited as she received the reply in her earpiece – but she looked perplexed. "Apparently there's no record of any Reynolds living on Avondale."

"It must be a mistake," Steve responded. "Jamie lives at number 11 with his parents."

Then all of a sudden, the officer stiffened as she listened intently to some more information filtering through her earpiece. In an instant, her entire body language had changed. She seemed perturbed as she quickly gathered her notes together. Her mind apparently now elsewhere, she said: "I've got to go now, but I'll come back later – OK?"

"OK. If you're sure you've got everything you need…" I said, feeling a little bemused.

"Thanks for your time," she told us, as we showed her to the door.

It didn't fall into place until much, much later, as Steve mulled over the many missing persons inquiries he'd been involved with, but the way she upped and left so suddenly was totally out of the norm. Usually, you could expect an officer to explain their next steps. And, of course, they'd tell you to get in touch if you heard anything yourself. But there was none of that. Looking back, it was as though whatever she'd heard on her radio had made our conversation irrelevant. Once again, things had shifted, escalated – and not long after the officer left, they took another turn.

Steve and I were, again, anxiously looking up and down the road from our bedroom bay window when the phone rang. It was Andy Murdoch, one of the detectives in Telford CID. We knew him well – Steve had actually tutored Andy when he was coming up through the ranks.

"All right, Steve," said Andy. "We're going to have a look at this. Tell me – is this the Jamie Reynolds with the weird hair cut?"

"Yeah – last time I saw him he had a big, floppy fringe, and fuzzy hair around the sides," Steve responded.

"OK. That must be him. We're going round there now to kick the door in. I'll get back to you."

At the time, the significance of that conversation went completely over my head. I was like a rabbit, dazzled by the glaring headlights of an oncoming truck. I didn't know which way to turn, couldn't think straight. Everything was moving so fast, swallowing me. But – for Steve – something had clicked. For the time being, he kept his concerns to himself. If I'd had my wits about me, I'd have been asking myself the same question as him: *Why have the police got a file and photo of Jamie?*

Just minutes after Steve hung up the phone, we heard the unmistakable, distant wail of police sirens. They grew louder – closer – by the second, obliterating the reassuring murmur of everyday life, just as our own lives – as we knew them – would soon be shattered.

Steve and I looked at each other: *What does this mean?*

"Will they be going to Jamie's?" I said, my nerves jangled by the drama and urgency of the police response.

"I think so," Steve replied, pausing for a moment. Then he added: "It's probably just because I'm a policeman – they want to do their very best."

Steve, I discovered later, was processing these new developments as Georgia's dad first, and as Detective Constable Williams second. *We don't kick doors in for missing person enquiries, not so soon,* he was thinking. But rather than worry me, and maybe because saying it out loud made it all the more real, he kept that thought to himself.

Instead, he said, "Keep an eye out over the road, I bet Georgia will come out of the park any minute!"

We kept up the vigil until – 20 minutes later – the phone rang again. It was Murdoch.

"OK, we've been to Jamie's and put the door in," he explained. "We've had a good search around the place. There's no sign of anything happening there – but no sign of the two of them either. Or Jamie's parents. The house is empty."

"What's next?" Steve asked.

"We're going to see if we can find him at work."

"All right," said Steve. "Thanks for the update. Let us know how you get on. You know where we are."

Relief flooded through me.

"That's good, isn't it?" I said. "She left Jamie's Sunday, went to the concert yesterday?"

Steve nodded. "It fits." Then he paused, thinking. "You don't think they've – you know – run off together?"

"Georgia and Jamie? No way!" I said. "She's with Matt. She'd never do that to him."

"No – you're right," Steve agreed. "That's not Georgia. That's not Georgia at all."

Without anything else to go on, we were clutching at straws. For the rest of the morning, we paced, and drank tea, between holding our breath waiting for the phone to ring. When it did, it was the police – announcing they needed to search our house. Three plain clothes officers arrived a short while later, lads from CID who Steve knew well. They shuffled in, looking more than a little embarrassed and obviously feeling awkward at having to search the home of a police colleague. "Sorry about this, Steve," one of them said. "It's just procedure, you know we've got to follow the script."

I couldn't help thinking: *Really? Do you honestly think you're going to find Georgia here? That we're making all this up for the sake of it? Or that we've done something to her?* It was degrading, humiliating, to feel like we were under suspicion. As they rummaged through our cupboards and wardrobes, poked under beds, I couldn't help wondering, *do they think it's us?* Of course, we knew we were completely innocent of any wrongdoing, that we were just ordinary parents who desperately wanted their daughter home safe and sound. We knew it – but did they? And more than that, it felt like such a waste of time and resources. Everyone could see we were worried sick. Why weren't they out there, looking for her?

We showed them Georgia's room, but it didn't offer any hiding places, other than under her double bed or in her wardrobe. Then one of the lads – wearing a shamefaced look – asked: "Have you got a ladder we can borrow? We need to get up in the loft."

Steve sighed resignedly. "Yeah, come on," he replied, and showed them the way.

As they rummaged around among the rafters, I said to Steve, "What are they up there for now? What's that all about?"

"You get cases where kids hide from their parents to scare them," Steve said. "Or someone will report a relative missing – but really they've killed them and hidden the body somewhere in the house."

"They can't possibly think we've done something like that to our Georgia!"

"I'm sure they don't," Steve soothed. "I don't like it either but they're just doing their job."

Over the years I'd been party to a bit of police procedure, but no one explained to us what was going on. I think they just assumed I'd automatically know, because my husband was a detective. When I calmed down, I told myself to tick it off as exactly that – procedure. Other parents who find themselves in similar situations to ours, without the understanding that comes from a police background, must feel so lost and scared. Your privacy, your integrity, are being invaded and questioned – yet you've done nothing wrong.

As the hours passed, other aspects of the police response added to our growing unease. The urgency of it all had taken us by surprise. Motorway gantries were lit up with a message asking for information about Georgia. A press release went out to the media. It was frightening. We were worried enough as it was, but the police were treating our concerns even more seriously than we'd expected. Georgia wasn't a wayward, vulnerable child – she was in her late teens. Under normal circumstances, she'd be considered low risk. We half thought the police would just turn around and say, "it's half term – she's rebelling against you. She's probably with friends. Give it a couple of days – she'll come home when she's ready."

But no. Instead, it was all systems go. And when Murdoch came back to let us know Jamie hadn't shown up for work, we called Scarlett to tell her we'd brought in the police.

"It's not like her at all," Scarlett said, worry creeping into her voice for the first time. "I'm coming over."

For now, it seemed the police were stumped. Jamie, even his parents, were nowhere to be found.

It was later that night as Steve, Scarlett, Maxine and I huddled in the front room together, with the TV droning on in the background, when Georgia's face flashed up on the screen. Both ITV and the BBC news were covering her disappearance.

"Oh my God!" I gasped, jolted by this new, grim significance.

It haunted me as I lay awake in bed that night, while Steve paced in his pyjamas downstairs, on sentry duty. And it was still in my head as we answered that 5.30am door knock to Detective Superintendent Adrian McGee and Chief Inspector Steven Tonks. We knew Adrian well. Just weeks earlier, we'd all been on a night out together at another officer's retirement do. Scarlett and Georgia had spent the whole night on the dance floor. We'd practically had to drag them away. Now, our carefree memories of pulsing disco lights and cheesy pop music were cast into deep shadow.

The way Tonks and McGee shuffled uneasily, shoulders slumped, uncomfortable in their own skins, spoke volumes. No doubt the fact we knew Tonks and McGee so well made it all the harder for them. They weren't simply police officers doing their job. They were friends, too. You had to feel sorry for them in a way. How does anyone find the right words for a situation like that?

"We've got something we need to talk to you about," McGee said. "Can we come in?"

SIX

Tonks and McGee sat on the sofa in our front room as Steve and I stood anxiously over them. They glanced nervously at each other, still struggling for words, uncertain who should go first. For what seemed like an age, no one spoke. I still had hope, but it was fading fast. My heart was pounding. Blood rushed in my ears. Pure dread was taking over.

Then McGee said: "We've found evidence on Jamie Reynolds' computer that makes us believe he's killed Georgia."

The words hit like a sledgehammer. It felt like every fibre in my body was screaming. And then I *was* screaming. Steve turned as white as a ghost. His stomach heaving, he clapped a hand over his mouth then ran from the room and threw up. As he returned, Scarlett came thudding down the stairs to find me yelling at Tonks and McGee, head in my hands: "Don't you say that! Don't you say that!"

"Mum? Dad?" Scarlett queried, her face collapsing.

We hugged her close and told her her sister was gone. But I was still shaking my head – *no-no-no*. I refused to believe, refused to allow this to be real. It wasn't happening to us, here in our front room. It was somewhere else. In a dream, or another reality.

"He's killed her, Lynnette!" Steve sobbed. "He's killed her!"

It just didn't make sense. Jamie was Georgia's friend, not some random stranger she'd encountered in the street. She was helping him. Why on earth would he kill her?

For now, all those questions would have to wait. We weren't ready for the answers. I felt a stab of rage, and over Scarlett's wounded screams I snapped at poor Tonks and McGee: "I think you'd better leave."

I said it like I meant it, jutting my chin at the door. Having two police officers sat on our sofa, even if they were friends, made this awful news all the more real. Some part of me thought if they weren't there, it wouldn't be true. But also, instinct was taking over. I just wanted to look after Scarlett and Steve. We needed to be alone, in our own space, to get our emotions out.

Quietly and respectfully, they nodded their agreement.

"For now, we need you to keep this between yourselves," McGee cautioned. "If anyone asks, Georgia's just missing. We're doing everything we can to locate Jamie Reynolds. We'll keep you updated."

We were alone with our tears. The next few hours passed in a haze, like we were in a surreal bubble. I can't say how or what we felt. It was like nothing I've felt before, or since. So many emotions – numbness, fury, gut-wrenching sadness, utter disbelief. For brief moments, when a lightness took over and my senses sharpened, there was even hope. *No – they've got it all wrong*, said a voice inside. *It's just a big mistake.* But then the walls would close in again, and a scream would gather inside me, twisting to be let out.

As soon as I reasonably could, I called social services, explaining what had happened. Our home was meant to be a place of safety and comfort for Maxine. We weren't fit to care for her with everything that was happening.

"This isn't the right place," I said. "Can you find another carer for today? Maybe longer. I don't know…"

They understood, and soon came round to take Maxine to a respite carer. It was someone I knew, which was a relief. I felt OK with that.

We spent the rest of the morning distraught. We cried, talked and hoped over endless cups of tea. No one even thought about food.

"They said they *believe* he's killed her," I offered. "That's not definite. And they said themselves Jamie's house was in order."

Steve shook his head. He'd been here before. Police officers don't knock on doors at half five in the morning unless they're absolutely certain.

"But if he's really killed her, where is she?" I said. "Something on Jamie's computer – what does that mean? How can they be so sure?"

But for now, Steve was focused on practicalities. We all cope in different ways and in that moment, ringing round the family was Steve's. He didn't want to panic anyone and risk them having a car accident on the way over, so he told them: "Can you pop round? We just want to get you all together so we can give you an update."

In the meantime, the news of Georgia's disappearance had reached her friends. Katy phoned us, desperate to help. Usually, she'd be calling to arrange a sleepover at ours. Countless times I'd walked in Georgia's bedroom to find the pair of them doubled over in laughter. They were both daft as brushes. But no one was laughing now. Katy rallied the community to help the police appeal for information.

Wellington has a real village feel to it and people living down this end of Telford have been here for years and years. Everyone knows everyone. Georgia's old school is five minutes' walk away. Cadets and New College are just down the road in Wellington town centre.

Georgia had touched people from all walks of life, even more than we realised. And now they wanted to give something back. With Katy at the helm, the kids were running around town putting posters up everywhere, and a local print shop let them run off as many as they needed, all for free. On Facebook, acquaintances from across the UK got in touch and shared news of the search.

But it was absolutely heartbreaking because we knew all their efforts were pointless. Katy was like our third daughter. She and Georgia were so close. But we had to keep the truth from her that Georgia was already gone, because the police had sworn us to secrecy. We had to play along and say the police just didn't know where she was. We had to pretend to be buoyed up by the kids' hope and enthusiasm. In a way, it was good for Georgia's friends because they felt they were doing something useful, but inside we just felt broken and helpless.

It was the same dreadful predicament with Matt. He came round to ours and wanted to be with us. He shared our pale-faced look of dread, because he knew Georgia going missing was so out of character. Like us, he was lost and couldn't comprehend how we were all in this position.

He sat with us for hours, talking and fretting, but we felt awful keeping secrets from him. It wasn't fair on any of us. We were torn – like Katy, he had a right to know, but at the same time we couldn't jeopardise the police investigation. The priority was tracking down Jamie and finding out what had happened to Georgia. In the end, we suggested Matt was better off at home with his mum and dad.

Soon, our relatives began arriving.

"Is everything OK, love?" my mum said as I showed her in.

"Let's wait for the others," I said. "We'll talk to everyone together."

We gathered in the front room again – my mum and dad, plus my foster brother and foster sister, Steve's brother, and also his sister and her husband. I don't know if they were expecting positive news. Going by our haunted faces and puffy, red eyes, probably not.

"We wanted to get you together before it comes out," Steve began, before his voice cracked. "We've had some news about Georgia – she's not coming back."

It felt like all the air had been sucked from the room as the enormity of Steve's words sank in.

Not coming back.

You could take it two ways, but everyone knew exactly what Steve meant.

I was numb, reeling with shock. I felt like an outsider looking in on some horrible play. We were surrounded by people we loved, and who loved us. But nothing they could say was going to make it any better, or any less real. And I had no answers for all their questions, not yet.

"There's one thing," I said. "For now, we have to keep it in the family. No one else can know. The police are looking for a boy called Jamie Reynolds. He's out there somewhere, and they're appealing to the public to help them find him."

"Is there any chance they've got it wrong?" someone asked.

"We can hope." I smiled thinly.

After that, I kept myself busy making tea for everyone. Anything to distract my mind. At one point, I came into the front room to find everyone glued to the TV news. Suddenly Georgia's face filled the screen again. Our Georgia, our daughter, in her beautiful blue prom dress.

"Police are appealing for…" the newsreader began.

But I couldn't stand it. "Turn it off," I snapped. "I don't want it on in the house!"

It wasn't long then before someone asked politely: "Shall we leave you on your own for a bit?"

With relief, I nodded. "If you don't mind."

They left, gobsmacked, in a flurry of hugs and tears, offering condolences and support.

We were still trying to process everything when there was another knock at the door. This time, one of the sergeants introduced two family liaison officers. They were both from CID, and – no offence – but it was obvious just from looking at them that they were hopelessly out of their depth.

They sat in the kitchen with us and didn't say a word. Just their presence made me feel uncomfortable, and I'm sure the feeling was mutual. Instead of looking after my family, or just getting to grips with my thoughts and emotions, I was busying about, making tea and coffee. I had to – just to break the oppressive silence bearing down on us. But I thought to myself, *I don't bloody need this. I've got enough to deal with, without having to look after this pair of lost sheep.*

I didn't understand who they were, or what their purpose was. No one had explained what they were meant to be doing. I'd assumed they were there to maybe give us a bit of counselling, or even just some support and comfort. There I was, tip-toeing around, actually looking after them, between answering the door to the parade of reporters who'd started knocking on the door. But it was Steve, Scarlett and I who needed looking after.

Certain people, you can't be emotional around, and I'd never met these two before in my life. They looked so blank. Even Steve, in his state of complete shock, was embarrassed for them. Scarlett was beside herself. I just wanted us to have our own space so we could talk things through and be emotional. I'm not usually like this, but it did get to the point where I felt they'd outstayed their welcome. There was nothing for it but to ask them to leave.

Finally, we had some peace and solitude. We were left alone. I was grateful for that because I'd rather any police manpower was directed to finding Georgia. Alone with our thoughts, we prayed together for some miracle that would bring her safely home to us. Even though we'd been given this awful news, we were clinging to the hope that it was wrong. Because we hadn't been given all the details, and because Georgia hadn't been found, our minds were filling in the blanks to create a happy ending. In desperation, we were praying that Georgia would be found safe and well.

After a while, we had the idea of going to a church. We're not regular churchgoers. We'd gone to occasional Christmas and Easter services over the years, but with Steve's work they'd become more infrequent. Now, maybe it felt like the prayers we were saying at home weren't enough, or perhaps we thought a show of faith would make it more likely they'd be heard.

We couldn't understand why God had allowed something so awful to happen to Georgia when she'd done nothing to anybody at all. Either way, we got in the car and drove, dumbstruck, to the Church of England church we'd been to in the past. Next to Scarlett in the back, the empty space where Georgia should have been sitting seemed huge.

We were oblivious to the radio puttering away in the background until, suddenly, Passenger's 'Let Her Go' came on. Both the girls had really taken this song to heart and I'd even found Georgia in her room jotting down all the lyrics so she could sing along to it. Hearing it like that just set us all off. It was uncanny, and the words captured just how we were all feeling.

Staring at the ceiling in the dark
Same old empty feeling in your heart
Love comes slow and it goes so fast

Well you see her when you fall asleep
But never to touch and never to keep

We all looked at each other, stunned, and Steve said: "That's Georgia just letting us know she's still with us."

We were upset to find the church locked and, in the end, we went to a Catholic church, St Patrick's, a mile or so up the road from us in Wellington. We desperately needed some guidance, and to talk to someone who wasn't connected to the police investigation. We found ourselves knocking on the priest's door, but at first he told us politely: "I'm sorry. I'm just with someone at the moment. Maybe later…"

"We just really need someone to talk to," I said. "It's our daughter, Georgia. She's gone missing. The police have told us they think she's been murdered. We're not Catholic, but − will you pray with us, and give us some peace and guidance. Please?"

"I see. Give me one minute," he said, disappearing inside the house.

He must have made his excuses because, not long after, his visitor left and he invited us in. We gathered in his sitting room and it was the most soothing space after the chaos of our home. There were times we'd felt like we were under invasion, with so many people coming and going, reporters knocking on the door.

We explained again the events of that morning, and the last couple of days, and he told us God was with Georgia, that he would protect her. He was such a lovely man and even though we'd never met him before he did make us feel a little bit better.

Afterwards, we went back into the church and Steve suggested, "Let's all light a candle for her."

Scarlett nodded. "That would be nice."

"Have you got a lighter? Or some matches?" I said.

None of us smoke, and after Steve patted down his pockets to find them empty, he said: "Hang on. I'll pop over the road to the pub."

We knew the Plough Inn well, as Georgia went there every May for their 'Our Heroes' fundraiser. With her keen interest in the military, it was an event close to Georgia's heart, and it was always packed. Kids would clamber over the armoured vehicle parked in the street outside. There were stalls, music and even a mini air display. Over the years they'd raised over £100,000 for various military charities.

Steve came back with a lighter and we lit our candles, saying our private prayers in silence. Comforting as it was in the church, we couldn't hide away in there forever. When we left, Steve ran ahead to the pub to give the lighter back. Scarlett and I followed him inside to find him slumped on one of the benches, staring at the TV, eyes filled with tears. Again, there was Georgia's face. It was another appeal on the news.

"Come on, Steve," I said gently. "Let's go."

But then the pub landlord, Ed Lowe, came over and asked: "What's up, mate?"

Steve gestured towards the TV. "That's our daughter."

For the second time that day, we were overwhelmed with the comfort and support of total strangers. Ed's wife, Ruth, gave me a hug and said, "It'll be OK, love." They brought out steaming hot coffee and sat chatting with us for the best part of an hour.

"I'm sure it'll be alright," Ed said, trying to reassure us. "Give it time, you'll see."

But it was hard to see past what the police had told us. "No – she's not coming back," we said.

Later, back at home, Steve Tonks called round with an update: they'd got Jamie.

"He was picked up in a hotel in Glasgow," he explained.

"Glasgow?!" I said, then felt a flash of hope. "Is Georgia with him? Have you found her?"

But it was soon extinguished as Tonks shook his head and explained: "He's claiming they arrived in Glasgow and went their separate ways."

"Rubbish," Steve scoffed. "With all this publicity, she'd have walked into the nearest police station and asked them to call her mum and dad to let us know she's safe."

"We've sent up a team to bring him back here. We'll know more when we get him in the interview room," Tonks replied.

Jamie's silver Toyota Hiace van had been picked up by the Automatic Number Plate Recognition system heading north. But what had really given Jamie away was using his credit card to check into a Premier Inn hotel. It immediately alerted the police to his location. Officers based in Glasgow had found him in his hotel room – but he was alone. His van was in the hotel car park.

"There was no sign of her?" I asked. "Clothes? Her handbag?"

Tonks shook his head. For now, they had nothing more to go on. Jamie was sticking fast to his story: after arriving in Glasgow, Georgia had gone off by herself and he'd decided to get a hotel room. For the time being, he'd been arrested on suspicion of kidnap. It was just a technicality, really, it didn't mean the police thought Georgia was still alive, just that without a body or enough other evidence they couldn't prove 100% that she was dead.

At some point, I went to bed and again lay there wide awake. Either my mind was racing at a hundred miles an hour trying to make sense of everything, or I was sobbing. Steve was back downstairs with his blanket, on sentry duty again at the front room window. He came upstairs at about 5am and we were sat talking when there was another early morning knock at the door.

It felt like a punch in the stomach because we knew it was bound to be more bad news. Again, it was Tonks and McGee.

They wanted us to look at a photograph. I glanced at it and looked away. The picture had been taken in the back of a panel van. Lying there on the cold, grubby, metal floor was a pink sock with little, round, bauble-type sweets. Just like the ones Georgia had been wearing when she'd left our house on Sunday.

"Lynnette," said Tonks. "Do you recognise this? Is it Georgia's?"

I knew it was, but I didn't say "yes" because I didn't want to admit it. Instead I shrugged, non-committal. "I'm not really sure."

"Do you want to look again?" Tonks suggested. "Steve?"

"I'm almost certain it's hers," Steve replied. "Come on, Lynnette. It's Georgia's."

I was going to break down, and I didn't want an audience. So I resorted to the now tried-and-tested method of asking the officers to leave us alone, which they did.

By now, Reynolds was in custody at Malinsgate police station awaiting questioning. If we still had any tiny shred of hope left after being shown that photo, the slow, drip-feed of information that came out of Malinsgate over the next couple of days would obliterate it completely.

The big question was – where was Georgia? She still hadn't been found, and Reynolds was keeping to his story. The police hoped the movements of Jamie's van might provide a clue, and they were asking for the public's help.

They knew it had left Wellington around noon on Monday and had arrived in Glasgow about 24 hours later. On the way, Reynolds had travelled via Oswestry, Rhyl, Chester and Kendal, and the van had also been spotted in Wrexham and Queensferry.

A *Crimewatch* reconstruction had been filmed, and it went out on TV that night. We couldn't bring ourselves to watch. It was hard enough dealing with the dreadful thoughts and images plaguing our own heads, without having to see them on the telly, too. But not long after it aired, the police had a breakthrough: someone phoned in to say they thought they'd come into contact with Reynolds on Monday night.

"We're searching a piece of land near Wrexham," Tonks told us. "Obviously, we've put this new information to Reynolds."

He couldn't say too much, but we got snippets of what was coming out in the interviews. Faced with this new evidence, Reynolds' story had changed. Like a child sat outside the headmaster's office, he now claimed he 'couldn't remember' what had happened from Sunday night onwards. He'd been poorly, he told detectives, and his mind was a blank.

Early the next morning, Friday May 31st, Steve's old police colleague – John Walker – came round. It was a relief to see someone we knew so well. John had volunteered to come and look after us, in a family liaison role. He's a good 20 years younger than Steve but we'd been to his wedding and knew his wife and kids. Straight away he knew what to say and how to say it. He was approaching this assignment as a caring friend rather than a job.

John explained how the location in Wrexham had been searched through the night. He reiterated what we'd already been told – that all the evidence so far suggested Georgia was dead. We could tell he was holding back, that he knew more than he was letting on. If we asked something that went beyond what he was allowed to tell us, he just nodded diplomatically and said: "Mmh – I'll have to get back to you on that."

To me, it was all a blur. We had so much to process, and at the same time we had to get our heads around the fact Georgia was gone. We were being told things, but it wasn't all going in because we were still in a state of deep shock.

In the meantime, our questions turned to how. How had Jamie killed her? What had he done to our precious daughter? Was it an accident? Had there been a fight? Had he forced himself on her, refusing to take no for an answer? And what about the texts we'd had from Georgia saying she'd headed off to a friend's?

John Walker was evasive at first, but it was his way of protecting us, making sure we weren't too overwhelmed. Georgia's messages had, of course, been sent by Jamie. Somehow he'd gained access to her phone. And John knew exactly what had happened to her, because while Jamie was claiming his own memory had conveniently been erased, his laptop and camera told the police the disturbing reality. They were filled with nightmarish memories of what had taken place at Avondale Road. Reynolds thought he'd been clever and deleted the evidence, but he was shocked when detectives told him they knew he'd killed Georgia – because the proof was still there on his devices.

The way John explained this proof to us took me a while to work out, and the thought of it will burden us for the rest of our lives. Georgia's last moments are just too awful to contemplate.

"He took some photos," John explained. "They're like – fantasy photos, special effects, so it appears as though Georgia's levitating or floating in the air."

I frowned, deep in thought.

Floating? What does he mean by floating?

Then Steve said: "She'd have fought back, John. She'd have put up a real good fight."

Steve's got a black belt in taekwondo. There'd been moments in his police career when it had stood him in good stead. But also, he'd passed on some of his self-defence skills to our two girls.

"She's strong," Steve continued. "There'll be forensic evidence. He'll be covered in scratches and bruises."

But I couldn't get those words out of my head: *Floating. Levitating.*

Then it dawned on me.

Steve was imagining Georgia in a fight with Reynolds, that she'd been killed in a struggle. And I was thinking: *No. She didn't even get the chance to put up a fight.*

"I've told the girls, if you're being attacked, you go for the eyes and the nose and the throat!" Steve said.

I shook my head. He hadn't twigged. "No, Steve," I said. "He's trying to tell you that Jamie's hanged her."

That's why Georgia appeared to be 'floating'. She was hanging from a rope – and Jamie was pulling the other end tight. He had actually lynched her and taken photos of her dying. I've never heard anything like it.

For a moment, it still didn't register with Steve, and then he broke down. He knelt on the floor at John's feet, pleading: "You get the fucking bastard. You get him. And you've got to find Georgia for us. Please find her!"

Tears sprang in John's eyes as he laid a hand on Steve's shoulder. "We will, Steve. We won't leave any stone unturned."

I was still taking it in and thinking about how much Georgia hated anything on her neck. It was a thing she had, not quite a phobia, but she wouldn't wear a polo neck jumper or even something with a tight collar. You only had to touch her neck and she'd flinch, pulling away from you with her chin tucked into her chest and her shoulders around her ears.

The idea of Reynolds putting a rope around her neck – she'd have absolutely loathed it. Any way to kill someone is just awful, but for Georgia, this would have been the worst thing imaginable. I found myself slipping back into disbelief.

This isn't true. It's not happening. She will be back.

It was a fight between reality – what had really happened – and what my mind would accept. When they say 'it's every parent's worst nightmare', it really is – but we'd just been taken way beyond that.

I wish I could say Georgia hadn't seen it coming, or that it had been quick and she wouldn't have suffered. But Reynolds had denied us even that tiny crumb of comfort. What he did was so callous and cruel, so calculated, it almost defies belief. Steve's been involved in plenty of murder investigations over the years. He's encountered crimes of passion, murder for revenge or for money, arguments that have got out of hand. Of course, taking any life is inexcusable. But what Reynolds did differed from all of those situations – because he killed just for the sake of killing. He killed purely to take pleasure in seeing someone die, revelling in their last moments. This is what sets Reynolds apart from most other murderers.

John came and went over the next few hours. He recognised we needed breaks, and there's no doubt in my mind that he needed them, too. Then at 2.30pm he came back with the news that you'd think we'd been absolutely dreading – but in fact it came as a huge relief.

"We've found Georgia," John said.

There are plenty of kids who go missing and are never found. I don't know how their parents cope, forever scanning the faces of people in the street, peering into dark alleyways, desperately clinging on to tissue-thin shreds of hope. I couldn't bear the thought of Georgia lying forgotten somewhere, at the mercy of the elements. We needed our girl home so we could say goodbye properly. At least now we'd have that. She hadn't been formally identified at that point, but they were sure.

"Can we see her?" I asked, eyes brimming.

"Not just yet. But – soon."

"Is everything with her? Her clothes – was she… wearing any clothes?" I asked, barely able to say the words.

John shook his head. "I'm sorry, Lynnette."

The spot she'd been found in was a lonely, desolate bit of woodland off the Nant-y-Garth pass, about ten miles northwest of Wrexham. The road is flanked by steep, wooded valley and John told us that without this call from the public, Georgia might never have been found.

The way Reynolds had been caught out sounded almost like a scene from some awful black comedy. He'd actually got his van stuck in the mud while he was looking for a place to dump our Georgia. A passing motorist had stopped to help push him out, and the guy's daughter had found the whole thing hilarious. She'd even taken photos of her dad pushing the van. When it appeared on *Crimewatch*, she'd recognised it instantly. Of course, she'd had no idea what was in the back.

I was overcome with rage. Reynolds had just shoved Georgia in his van, naked, and driven around looking for somewhere to throw her out. She was still young and self-conscious about her body. The thought of her being violated in that way sickened me. He'd shown her zero respect or compassion and instead treated her like a piece of meat.

We'll be forever grateful for that call to *Crimewatch* because otherwise it'd have been us peering into those dark alleys and staring at strangers, hoping, for the rest of our lives.

Now, all we could hope for was justice. Jamie Reynolds had run out of excuses. He was charged with Georgia's murder.

SEVEN

Steve and I sat together in our bedroom bay window. It had been the scene of so much hope in the past week, as we'd peered out eagerly, eyes scanning the street outside, looking for some sign of our Georgia – a flash of her red hair as she turned the corner, a black smudge of leather jacket. But she was never coming home. Instead, a police officer stood sentry by the cordon at the end of our road, the last line of defence against the endless stream of reporters and TV cameras.

I felt under siege, boxed in. I didn't want to be caught unawares saying something I didn't really mean. I couldn't face having microphones stuck under my nose when I was least expecting it. We felt like we were living in a completely different world. One where we were incapable of thinking straight. One where it would have been all too easy to say the wrong thing.

We'd had reporters' business cards and even thick, heavy media packs from press agencies shoved through the door. We'd ignored practically everyone except the local paper and the regional BBC reporter. I felt as though they were on our side, helping us tell the town about Georgia. Telford locals genuinely shared our loss, because so many had known her. Georgia was one of them. If we gave the *Shropshire Star* a photo, we knew it would have real, emotional meaning to its readers. By comparison, the fevered attention from some of the national newspapers felt intrusive. We'd become just another story to sensationalise, with garish headlines and photographs of Jamie Reynolds.

Every time I saw one, my chest hitched and the band of white rage cinched around my heart tightened a little more. My hate for that boy burned in every cell of my body. And there was one particular photo that the papers had found on his Facebook of him and Georgia together which just cut me to the core. It almost made it look as though they were a couple, laughing and joking together like a pair of young lovebirds – when in fact nothing could have been further from the truth. I didn't want people thinking they were boyfriend and girlfriend, certainly didn't want people remembering Georgia in that way, because it belittled what happened to her.

We were alone now in the house for the first time in days, and the last in what would be weeks. Even Scarlett had fled to Jadine's for a few days, struggling to cope with the overwhelming pressure of mine and Steve's sadness. All hope was gone. The quiet smothered us like a freezing wet blanket.

The mountain of damning evidence the police had found on Jamie's computer and in his house meant we'd known he'd be charged eventually. He simply had to be, it was just a matter of time. Yet somehow it still came as a shock. I felt relieved in one way that the police had found the perpetrator, but also stunned it was someone Georgia had known and trusted. Someone who'd sat at the end of the drive with his engine idling, waiting for her and her mates to grab their coats. Someone we'd exchanged pleasantries with countless times after filling up the car at the garage down the road. Someone Georgia had stuck up for and counted as a friend.

My mind drifted. I could scarcely believe this was happening to us. I didn't want it to be. Then a thought bubbled to the surface. Football? Something to do with Telford United? I grasped for meaning through the fog clouding my brain – then found it. We'd known for a while now that Georgia was gone, but the wider community had only learned the truth when Jamie was charged. Now I remembered my sister Lesley telling me friends and well-wishers were planning to gather at Telford United. New Bucks Head stadium was the natural place to hold a remembrance, and for people to begin to make sense of their – and our – loss. Georgia had such happy times there, working the crowds with my dad or cheering on the players from the commentary box. She was part of the Bucks family, and it was the one place in town that could accommodate her wide circle of friends, alongside everyone else whose lives she'd touched in some way.

I explained to Steve what was planned, and said: "Should we go?"

"Mmh?" he said, lost in thought.

"This remembrance. Should we go?"

I wasn't 100% sure. We were still in shock and I didn't know if I was ready to be surrounded by people, everyone looking at us. We'd barely had a moment to be alone with our thoughts and process what had happened. It had been such a whirlwind. We really needed some peace.

But maybe it will help? I wondered. "Perhaps we should," I offered, still uncertain. "See the flowers…"

"OK," Steve agreed, still in a daze. We felt like we were moving through treacle. The world was in soft focus, our emotions frayed.

Scarlett met us at the ground and the three of us picked our way along the terraces, where scarves and football shirts had been knotted to the railings. I stooped to read some of the messages pinned to bouquets of flowers or accompanying the cuddly toys and little trinkets left in tribute to Georgia.

Thank you for being the best friend.
I was so lucky to have you in my life.

We'll never forget you, Georgia.

People expressed how sad they were, others said Georgia had been such a beautiful person. She was described as funny, caring, and unforgettable.

The end stand of the ground was packed with people, disbelief and bewilderment etched on their faces. Others came and went – laying more flowers, stammering over their condolences.

"You OK, love?" I said to Scarlett, reading the hurt in her tightly drawn features. As people pressed their hands to hers, I sensed she was struggling to hold it together. She swallowed hard and nodded. The whole experience was overwhelming.

Again, I was in a daze. In the back of my mind, I knew Jamie was appearing in a magistrates' court somewhere, charged with murder. But it was just a formality – the case would be kicked up to Crown Court. And anyway, today was about Georgia.

I remember at one point a uniformed policeman making a beeline for me to say hello. He was tall, clean cut, with a good head of short, blond hair and a warm, open face. From his spiel and the way he carried himself, he came across as a management level officer. It turned out Steve had actually met him at work once before, when he'd borrowed some equipment off him for a job. He shook my hand as he introduced himself. Inspector Richard Langton.

"Call me Dick," he said. "Everyone calls me Dick."

I also remember Telford United's anthem, 'Keeping the Dream Alive', by Freiheit, booming out over the tannoy. Steve wrapped a protective arm around me as my tears flowed. Matt, hunched in the terraces in front of us, held his head in his hands and sobbed. He had plenty of company – there was barely a dry eye in the stadium.

"I really should thank everyone for coming," Steve said, gazing around him.

He was actually thinking of walking around the stadium, going person to person to thank them all one by one. But then a guy from the club came over and said: "There's a microphone out on the pitch."

Steve followed him over, but someone had got their wires crossed – literally. I was too shell-shocked to realise Steve's speech wasn't being broadcast by tannoy to the crowd. Although he teetered on tiptoes to address the stands, in fact his microphone and his speech were plugged into a BBC news feed.

"I'd like to thank everybody who's here for coming down and showing their love for Georgia," Steve said, looking straight into the stands as he fought tears. "She was into everything. She was a great girl. Everybody think of her. Never say 'she was', say 'she is'. Talk about her as though she's here and always will be here with us. I'm just going to end by saying, Georgia you were a great girl. Thank you for being in my life. God bless you."

In the days that followed, there were more of the formalities you read about in the papers when someone is murdered, or loses their life in some tragic way. But now we were at the heart of it.

Phrases like 'identified by dental records' and 'post mortem examination' and 'inquest has been opened' reached us either through the myriad members of West Mercia Police beating a path to our door and camped out in our living room, or via the local newspaper. I didn't need little bits of paper, or pathologists, or coroners to tell me that Georgia was dead, and that Jamie Reynolds had hanged her. That much we knew with absolute certainty, but there was one huge unknown that plagued me every time I closed my eyes – this bit of woodland where Georgia's body had been found.

We knew it was somewhere off the A525 to Ruthin in Wales, a winding bit of road called the Nant-y-Garth pass, but beyond that we didn't really have a clue where it was. In my head, I had horrible visions of a dark, damp forest, miles from anywhere. As I said, I've got this thing about worms, and in my rare snatches of sleep, I had nightmares of our Georgia lying in the woods with all the creatures having a go at her. I'd wake with a gasp thinking, *what a bastard to just dump her there like that.* The way he'd killed her was awful enough, but how degrading for poor Georgia to be treated so callously afterwards, rolling around in the back of his van, dumped, abandoned. To come to that end, and then to be discovered – naked – by police and forensic examiners poring over her, scrutinising the scene. I found that especially hard to deal with – still do – because Georgia was quite prim and proper in that way. I hate Jamie Reynolds for everything he did to Georgia, but – if it's possible – I hate him even more for that. He utterly dismissed her as a human being.

"If you'd like to go, it can be arranged," John Walker told us. "I'll drive you there myself. You could lay some flowers."

"I don't know," I said with a sigh. I was unsure. I did want to go – and I didn't.

I knew I had to find some way of laying to rest the awful visions I was having. Without knowing what this place was really like – seeing it and feeling it for myself – my mind filled in the gaps for me, and in the worst possible way. But on the other hand, what if I got there and it was even worse than I'd imagined?

"Of course, it's your decision," said John.

Steve was in two minds as well. We mulled it over for a couple of days before telling John: "If you don't mind, we'd like to go."

It was a bright day when Steve and I set off from Telford, sat in the back seat of John's car, a bunch of roses between us on the seat. It felt like the beginning of summer. The warmth and sunshine did nothing to soothe my nerves, though. I felt apprehensive and sick to my stomach. We drove west through Shrewsbury in near silence. On to Oswestry and then over the border into Wales. I was

113

in disbelief that this is what our lives had come to – sat in the back of a police car on our way to lay some flowers where our dead daughter had been dumped by her murderer. John didn't attempt any small talk either. He knew us well enough for that, and I'm certain he felt awful, too. Only a couple of weeks earlier he'd been dancing with our girls at the same retirement party Adrian McGee had attended. He'd known Georgia since she was little.

The towns gave way to countryside as we plunged into the wilds of the Welsh borders. The pass cut through a steep, wooded valley following the Nant-y-Garth river, the road criss-crossing across the water in a number of places. The hillside to the right was lined with tall, stringy pine trees. On the left there was dense forest and high banks covered in hedge. We passed rocky outcrops and mounds of shale that looked ready to slip from the hillside onto the tarmac.

It's a miracle she was found at all, I pondered. I couldn't help wondering whether her missing clothes, handbag and phone were out there somewhere, discarded in the undergrowth.

The hour and a quarter drive felt like forever. Then we turned a corner and there on the left was a gravel layby, with a police patrol car parked in it. *This is it,* I thought.

John pulled into the layby, and Steve and I climbed out of the car. By the side of the road, bunches of flowers lay in a neat line. I hadn't realised people had gone to the bother of driving out here to lay flowers. It was a touching gesture.

"This way," said John, leading us to the back left corner of the layby, where a steep, rutted track climbed among more stringy pines. It was muddy underfoot and I could see how Jamie had managed to get the van stuck fast in the slop. If he hadn't, this place would never have been found. The track climbed for about 150 yards where it reached open countryside. But before that – on the left – was a small clearing leading to a wooded area.

We pushed in among the trees and found the spot where Jamie had dumped Georgia – a little hollow among fallen logs. It clearly hadn't been touched in years. Unless you were felling trees, there was no real reason to come here at all.

I laid the flowers down and Steve and I sat on a log, saying very little. It was bright, with sunbeams angling in between the leaves and a note of warmth in the air. The gurgle of the brook below reached our ears. Today – luckily – it wasn't the dark, cold, scary place I'd summoned in my nightmares.

"I think Georgia would have liked it here," I said.

Steve nodded. "It's nice. She wouldn't have been frightened by it."

"You can imagine her camping here with her mates."

We sat for a while longer, lost in our own thoughts, and after about half an hour we made our way back to the road where John was waiting to take us home.

"I feel a bit calmer about that," I said. "It's nicer than I'd imagined." Then we drove home – again, almost in silence. I remember we returned to the woods perhaps a few months later to plant a shrub, but that was the last time. And I wouldn't go again. It'd trigger too many awful memories, and it makes me so angry that Jamie just dumped Georgia there.

Meanwhile, back at home, Georgia's friends had been busy remembering her in their own way. A lad from college, Steve Millington, had set up a fundraising page for donations. He wanted to put a memorial bench in Bowring Park. He'd been deluged with support and had the £1800 in no time. Money was still pouring in. College friends and businesses were selling wristbands in Georgia's memory, made in her favourite colours – orange and turquoise. The plan was to donate any surplus to a charity.

The kids were doing so well, they even attracted the attention of the police – Inspector Dick Langton, to be precise. We were used to police officers coming and going at all hours of the day, and now that Jamie had been charged, the to and fro resumed. At first I thought Dick was just part of the circus, but he had something else on his mind when he turned up on the doorstep, unannounced. We invited him in and he explained he was an inspector at Wellington police station.

"I'll be involved in organising the crowds for the funeral," he said.

That word, *funeral*. I hadn't properly thought about it. Arranging a funeral for your own child – it's just heartbreaking.

"OK," I said. "Thank you."

"There's something else… I know some of Georgia's friends have been fundraising. I'm just a bit wary about young students being left in control of all that money."

I thought he perhaps had a point. By now, there was over £2100 in the pot and it was still rising.

"I think we need to give some thought to the surplus," Dick said. "What's going to happen with it?"

I hadn't considered it. It was the last thing on my mind.

"The kids were thinking of donating it to a charity. Have you got another idea?" I said.

"Well – it needs to be handled in an organised way. I wondered – why don't *we* set up a charity?"

We? I thought. I could barely tie my own shoelaces at the time. The only way I could get any sleep was by popping a tablet, and I had Georgia's funeral to organise.

Maybe he caught the look on my face, because he said: "I can handle it. Put everything in place."

In that case, why not? I thought. Right now, we just needed a safe place for the excess money. In time, we could use it to create a fitting legacy for Georgia. I nodded. "That sounds good. And thank you. Just let me know if you need anything from us."

"Not at all – *you* let *me* know if you need anything for the funeral. I'll be in touch."

That word again. *Funeral.* Our daughter's funeral. It was unfathomable. We had to arrange our daughter's funeral.

I'd got it in my head that I didn't want it morbid, or dark. I wanted light and colour. Even though Georgia's life had been short, I wanted her funeral to be a celebration of that life. I know people often say that, but with Georgia I felt like we had to make the effort, because she really did celebrate living.

I can't remember who it was, but I recall telling someone how I wanted to tie ribbons in Georgia's favourite colours all along the route to the church.

"What are you doing that for?" this person said.

I burst into tears of anger. "I'm just doing the best I possibly can for Georgia – now – because unfortunately, I won't be helping with a wedding, or christening or anything else like that! It's all been taken away. I don't want to do this! Why would anyone *want* to do this? But I have to make it the best I can!"

We had a lot of help. By chance, a close friend of mine, Linda, worked at the local funeral parlour. She knocked on the door one day and said: "I'll be handling it – you just ring me for anything at all. Nothing is too much trouble."

There was a specific coffin I wanted for Georgia, made of wicker so it had an earthy, natural look. I wanted it covered in blue flowers, and we suggested everyone who planned to come on the day wear whites and more bright blues.

Steve and I discussed what Georgia should be dressed in. There were a few cherished dresses that we could have picked. But really there was only one choice.

"It's got to be her uniform," Steve said.

I agreed. Georgia had had the best times of her life down at that air cadets hut, or away on camps and exercises with her young comrades. She'd put hours into it, rising to the rank of corporal before she was killed. She'd been on the cusp of signing up for real. It was her dream – the RAF would have been her life. Georgia always looked immaculate in her uniform, and she'd do it proud one last time.

When I retrieved it from her wardrobe, it looked pristine. Her shoes were still polished. Tony Skelding – a sergeant from Steve's work – had offered to take the uniform to the funeral parlour for us, because we couldn't face the outside world. Handing it over felt so final. It was like giving away a piece of Georgia – what she'd been and what she certainly would have one day become.

In the daze and confusion of our grief, there was plenty we hadn't considered, but there was no shortage of people to step in and help out. We hadn't really envisioned how many would want to come and say their final farewells – a mark of how many lives Georgia touched – and the police suggested we'd need a sound system outside the church, plus projector screens inside. Local businesses offered them free of charge. We hadn't given any thought to food, until Telford United stepped in and offered to lay on a buffet and open the bar. Tony Skelding liaised backwards and forwards on managing the route we'd follow in the cortege. A lot of it was taken out of our hands. We were swept along.

It was now two weeks since we'd smothered Georgia in kisses and stood on the doorstep to wave her goodbye. We decided between us that we wanted to see her one last time, a decision that fills me with regret to this day. The sombreness of a chapel of rest was just completely at odds with the energy and vitality that everyone knew Georgia for.

"I want to come," Scarlett said.

"Are you sure?" I asked.

I was in two minds whether it was the best idea for her. In the last couple of years, the girls had grown so close, and the five-year age gap between them seemed to matter less and less. But Scarlett nodded. Mum and Dad wanted to come, too, so we drove to the funeral director together, unsure exactly what to expect but knowing we were counting down the minutes to one of the most difficult moments of our lives.

My friend Linda had told me before: "We've tried to make Georgia look like Georgia as best we can." They'd done all they could to hide the damage animals had done to her while she'd laid in the woods, but I still wanted to shield Scarlett from whatever lay beyond the door to the chapel of rest until I'd seen for myself.

"We'll go in first," I told Scarlett, Mum and Dad. "Just wait there a minute and you can go in after."

Steve and I pushed through the door. Piped music trickled in, adding to the sombre tone. At the end of the room was the wicker coffin I'd chosen for Georgia. I felt sick as Steve and I approached it, and when I saw over the lip of the coffin, a wave of pain and nausea hit me and I let out a howl. It just wasn't Georgia at all. Yes – it was a young woman with flame red hair, dressed in an immaculate air cadet's uniform. But our Georgia? Surely not. This girl looked like she'd been battered about. Her colour was wrong. And although the funeral parlour had tried, there was no disguising the effects of the elements or the wildlife. It was absolutely horrendous. My hysterical screaming was answered from the corridor outside by something like an echo as I set Scarlett off too.

A couple of minutes passed before I managed to get my sobs under some semblance of control, then Steve and I stood there, holding hands, hugging each other, and crying.

"Why did this have to happen to her?" I said.

Steve shook his head, lost for words.

We laid some family photos in the coffin with her, and Steve leaned in to give her a kiss. I couldn't bring myself to do it, and instead stroked her hand. After saying one last goodbye we returned to Scarlett, Mum and Dad, waiting outside. Scarlett was still sobbing. Mum and Dad's faces were creased with concern. As Scarlett – half blinded by tears – scrabbled for the door handle, Steve stopped her.

"We don't think you should go in," he said.

Scarlett looked at him questioningly.

"Come on," Steve said, gently trying to lead her away.

Scarlett screamed and wheeled around, trying to push past him to the door, but Steve barred the way.

"Trust us, Scarlett. Just remember her as she was," I said, before turning to Mum and Dad. "And you, too."

Later, I spoke to my friend, Linda. "If anyone else asks to see Georgia, please tell them 'no'. It's too upsetting." I thought it was better for friends and family to remember Georgia as crazy and vivacious, with an infectious, silly laugh than for their last memory to be of her cold and still in that coffin.

Not long after John Walker had driven us out to Nant-y-Garth, he came round for a chat and asked if we'd mind if he withdrew from his liaison role. The poor guy looked like he'd aged about five years in the last week, and his profound sadness was written all over his face. The fact he'd been so close to us – and to Georgia – for so many years had got the better of him.

"We totally understand," Steve told him, as John explained how Tony Skelding would be taking over from him. Steve meant it – he really did understand. We both did. It must have been so hard for John being there with us as our world unravelled. We were grateful he'd tried. I still don't know how we got through those few weeks ourselves. A lot of it, I've probably blocked out just so I can keep a fingertip hold on my sanity. Steve was in a constant state of shock. I was trying to keep it together for Scarlett's sake, because she was still young herself. What I do know is that we never really had the time, the space or the silence to process what was happening.

Once Jamie had been charged, the police investigation swung into action – and Steve unwittingly found himself at the heart of it.

Every day, the police had something new to tell us, or they wanted Steve's advice. A constant stream of officers came and went from the house, bringing with them a whirlwind of information.

I remember waking each morning and thinking *I'll just get through today somehow.* And then I'd sit on the sofa as another officer pounded us with more information. I couldn't take any of it in. The band of concrete encasing my brain was impenetrable.

I want to scream, I thought. *I want to scream, and to run out of this house. I want to get Jamie, and I want to kill him.* I'd given a lot of thought to killing Jamie Reynolds, and I'd decided I could quite easily do it. It'd be just what he deserved, and the world would be a better place without him.

For Steve, it was even worse. People seemed to have forgotten he was a grieving dad. They couldn't see past the police badge. Already weighed down with his grief and shock, Steve was being burdened with the investigation, too. He was being treated almost like a member of the team, an officer in the case. The torment of trying to get through the day, and process case information on top, was too much for him. He felt responsible. He had to maintain the stiff upper lip. He felt that if he made a mistake everything would go wrong. He hated it when people cut corners. Which is why it hurt so much when Steve Tonks and Adrian McGee turned up at the house, once again shuffling uncomfortably as they steeled themselves for delivering more bad news. We'd had an inkling that Jamie Reynolds was known to the police, because they had his photo on file, and they'd wasted no time busting into his house. But at this stage, we still didn't know the half of it.

"Steve, Lynnette, we've got something we need to tell you about Reynolds," Tonks began. "He's been dealt with by the police before, and unfortunately not very well."

"What do you mean, 'not very well?'" I said. "Dealt with how?"

"We've had to send a referral to headquarters," Tonks said. He was struggling to contain his anger – and then he let it go. "People are going to lose their fucking jobs over this."

"What was he dealt with for?" Steve asked. "What did he do?"

"He attacked a girl."

EIGHT

The expressions on Tonks' and McGee's faces veered between unease and anger. Their revelation suggested the police might have known what Jamie was capable of. But why didn't the community know? Or the girls he'd gone to college with? Steve and I were furious.

"When is this supposed to have happened?" I asked. "Who did he attack?"

McGee shook his head. "We can't…"

"Well – how did he get away with it? You must know something!"

We needed answers. I was sure they knew more than they were letting on, but they were bound by procedure. For now, they had to play their cards close to their chests.

"All we can tell you at this stage is that there was a prior incident where he attacked a girl," Tonks told us.

It was so bitterly ironic. Steve had always gone above and beyond to do a good job. He had the framed commendations to prove it. I thought of all those times he'd arrived home late, long after we'd gone to bed, and how we'd wake in the morning to discover he'd already left for work, barely able to rest until he'd cracked the case. And now it sounded like Georgia had lost her life in the most awful way imaginable, all because someone couldn't be arsed to do their job properly.

"What happens now?" I said, throwing my hands up in disgust. Whatever it was, it would never be enough. It was never going to bring Georgia back.

"Like we said, it's been referred," McGee explained. "But we're going to get to the bottom of it."

We tried pushing for more information, but it was futile. Steve and I were left to absorb yet another devastating blow. If it was possible, the hole in our lives had just got even bigger.

We were determined that one day there would be a reckoning, but for now our focus had to be on Georgia, and giving her the best send-off possible. Over the next few days, I delved into all the old photos of our family adventures over the years. I'd hoarded pictures religiously, and they told the story of Georgia's life right from when she was a little baby. There were thousands of images, either arranged neatly in family albums with labels like 'America' and 'Lanzarote Holiday' written on their spines, or stacked in plastic boxes waiting to be filed away. I'd driven the girls mad when they were little, forever lining them up for pictures so I could capture treasured moments on film. But I was so glad now that I'd persisted. All I had left of Georgia were memories and photos.

I thumbed through the pictures and tacked them to a display board I'd borrowed from the school. Knowing there would be no more was gutting.

I started at the beginning, when Georgia was born, with pictures of a cute, chunky little baby, through all her exploits growing up, and finished with photos of a beautiful teenager blossoming into early adulthood. Georgia was still tiny, still short, but she was beginning to get the face and figure of a woman. She was leaving childhood behind. And there, her story ended. It was heartbreaking.

Steve had decided to wear his police uniform to the funeral, complete with white parade gloves. For my part, I wanted something light and bright. I couldn't face the town centre shops, but one of the outlets on the retail park had a late opening night. Knowing it would be quiet, and confident that we could slip in and out, away from prying eyes, Scarlett and I headed up there. I picked out a dress in royal blue, and Scarlett found something in white with a blue floral print. Going clothes shopping for a funeral felt an odd thing to do, and it was yet another painful reminder of happy times when the four of us had hit the shops together.

In the meantime, my mum had got the local flower shop to order some spools of ribbon in orange and turquoise. The evening before Georgia's funeral was warm and bright, and we went out together as a family to tie bows on the lampposts along the route of her final journey, just as I'd planned. I wanted to make it pretty for her, and although I drew some comfort from doing this simple, little thing, it was tinged with the absolute disbelief that I was having to do it all.

We'd been in our own bubble since Georgia had gone missing, but as we tied the ribbons, a few friends I hadn't seen in a while stopped their cars to chat and say how sorry they were. Steve was just wrapping one around a lamppost as a man came up to him to offer his condolences. It turned out he was an ex-prisoner who'd just been released from a six-year sentence. He'd had his fair share of run-ins with the police, and he knew Steve from old.

"Mr Williams, I heard about your daughter," he began. "You know I hate the police…"

"Yeah, I know you hate the police," Steve said.

"Well – nonetheless I just wanted to say how sorry I am. It's awful what happened to her. I really am sorry."

They say there's honour among thieves, and it seemed even hardened criminals had been touched by Georgia's dreadful fate.

The day itself was surreal. I got up in a daze after barely any sleep, desperate to just get it over with. We couldn't face breakfast, and I got dressed on autopilot before relatives began arriving to be picked up in the funeral cars.

As the hearse pulled into our close, I felt a flood of panic. *It's happening. This is really happening,* I thought. I tried to pull myself together. *Remember – we're doing this for Georgia.*

Scarlett, Steve and I climbed into one of the three waiting cars, and we set off for the church.

The route went up the road from the house, and past Georgia's old school where kids and teachers had gathered outside the gates to show their respect. It was the same down King Street at New College, with fellow students standing out front as we drove by in the cortege. Over the road at the HQ of 1130 Wrekin Squadron, Georgia's cadet comrades had formed a guard of honour, and after we'd passed them, they set off marching to the church. It was touching to know they felt the same way about her as she did about them. There were locals, friends and neighbours all along the route to wish Georgia well on this last voyage. I caught the eye of one old colleague from Boots, a woman I'd helped through losing her husband in unexpected, tragic circumstances years earlier. Her expression acknowledged our mutual loss. She understood what we were going through.

We drove on past New Bucks Head stadium and then into Wellington town centre to All Saints Parish Church. Our cortege stopped for nothing – four police motorbike outriders secured each junction in advance, holding up the traffic so we could cruise through red lights and crossroads. Then they zoomed past us to do the same at the next junction. The whole thing had been organised like a royal visit. Georgia had lived her life at full throttle. Never resting. Never stopping. Now she had brought the town to a standstill.

I gasped as we pulled into the yard at the back of the church and caught sight of the sea of agonised faces. I hadn't expected so many people. They filled the yard and spilled out onto the street right up to the shops. Air cadets from all over the country were lined up in a long chain, arms linked in a show of solidarity and looking immaculate in their uniforms. People were dressed in bright colours, with lots of blues and oranges, just as we'd asked. A circular bench on the church forecourt was laden with bunches of flowers.

We got out of the cars and gathered around the hearse, Scarlett and I linking arms and propping each other up for support. People began to file into the church. RAF top brass from Cosford had come down to pay their respects. David Shaw, the Chief Constable of West Mercia Police, was there too. Even the local MP, Mark Pritchard. A squad of police cadets marched in, side-by-side in pairs. The church bells rang out and a hush fell over the crowd standing waiting on the yard outside. Steve stepped up to help carry Georgia inside – it wasn't something we'd talked about, but in the moment it seemed the natural, fatherly thing to do.

The church only held 450 people and there must have been at least double that number, so the rest listened to the service outside, relayed by loudspeaker. As I took my seat on the wooden pew, I noticed the air cadets lined up proudly down the side of the church. We'd asked for the service to start with 'All Things Bright and Beautiful', because Georgia was both – and it suited her to a tee.

Steve had wanted to say a few words, and by chance the vicar had dropped a poem off at the house written by some of Georgia's college friends. He'd given it a quick read through and decided it was perfect. He stepped up to the front and began:

"We thought of you today,
but that is nothing new.

127

We thought of you yesterday,
and the days before that too.
We think of you in silence.
We often speak your name.
Now all we have is memories,
and your picture in a frame.
Your memory is our keepsake,
with which we will never part.
God now has you in his keeping Georgia,
but we all have you in our hearts."

I sat there, clinging to Scarlett, and quietly crying. I couldn't bring myself to look around the church and instead stared straight ahead, or at the huge photo of Georgia displayed on the screens. It was overwhelming.

At one point, the Reverend Mark Ireland addressed the congregation and talked about making Wellington a better, safer, more caring place. Telford had been making headlines for all the wrong reasons recently due to the child grooming scandal, and now the town had been rocked by losing Georgia in a way no one could quite comprehend. Reverend Ireland hoped this loss might rally the town to rekindle its community spirit.

"In years to come people will remember Georgia's tragic death as a turning point, a moment of hope, the moment when Wellington rediscovered its soul," he said.

Then we had a friend of Georgia's from college – Dan Crossley – play a song he'd composed himself. There was a nervous anticipation as his footsteps echoed around the church before he took a seat at his keyboard. The second his fingers struck the keys, he just blew us all away. I couldn't believe how good he was, it was like having Elton John in the church. Dan had been inspired to write 'Georgia's Song' shortly after she'd gone missing, while there was still some hope of a happy ending, and it was really his way of just asking her to get in touch and let us know she was OK. "I hope you're still wrapped up at night, I hope you feel just fine," he sang. "I hope your heart still beats in time."

The lyrics still made perfect sense to me, because wherever she was now, I wanted her to be safe and warm.

Georgia's old high school teacher, Mary Parry-Sargeant, said a few words. She'd been the driving force in getting the Boeing plane project off the ground. She revealed they'd be naming the plane after Georgia when it was finally complete. "Every time it flies a part of her will take to the skies," she said.

Chay Davis, her old headteacher, told us how Georgia had blown him away in her interview for head girl by gathering glowing letters of recommendation from members of staff. She'd sat down with him to discuss all the issues she wanted to address if she was picked for the job. "I knew before she walked out of the door that she'd got it," he said.

As the service was drawing to a close, Reverend Ireland turned to look at me, Steve and Scarlett, and said: "You are not alone in bearing this loss. We cannot stand in your shoes, because we have not lost what you have lost, but we can stand next to you, and we will do so, not only today but in the months and years ahead."

I felt a wave of relief that it was coming to an end. I just wanted to get out of there. Steve stepped up again to help carry Georgia's coffin back to the hearse, and we filed back outside to Freiheit's 'Keeping the Dream Alive'.

From the church, we went on to the crematorium – family only this time. Maxine – bless her – had put on her own cadet uniform to stand in unity with the others in church. She wanted to be with us and arranged for her social worker to bring her up to the crematorium. The service there felt totally different to church. Away from the glare of the cameras and the overwhelming feeling of hundreds of people looking at me, it was more intimate. I felt less on edge.

We played Bon Jovi's 'Livin' on a Prayer', and I thought of the times Georgia had used that song to give a boost of encouragement to younger cadets clinging terrified to some rockface. Georgia would be at the bottom, holding the rope, and singing: "Woah – you're halfway there!" Singing this cheesy song would defuse their fright, their fears dissolving into laughter. More often than not, they'd finish the climb.

Then there was Passenger's 'Let Her Go', which always seems so apt for Georgia. Hearing it always conjures a mix of sadness and comfort. It never fails to bring tears to my eyes, but I'm sure it's Georgia's way of letting us know she's near.

Steve and Maxine went up to the front together and gave Georgia a last salute. I felt devastated. In the flesh, our Georgia was gone. As 'You've Got a Friend In Me' from *Toy Story* began playing, we filed out of the crematorium.

"I'll just be a moment," said Steve, stood by Georgia's coffin.

"We'll see you outside," I said.

Georgia had grown up with the *Toy Story* films, and she'd adored that song. She had the Woody doll, and as I sat in the car waiting for Steve, I recalled the times we'd laughed as we all sang the words together.

After the tears and heartache of the funeral service, the wake back at New Bucks Head felt more like a celebration of Georgia's tragically short life. There were still times I struggled to shake the feeling that we were trapped on an unstoppable, runaway train, moving from one stage of the funeral to the next – without a moment to have a private cry or just reflect on things. But I knew everyone's heart was in the right place.

People gathered around the photo collage I'd made, the pictures from Georgia's younger years sparking memories and conversation. One of her friends had spliced together a compilation of clips from all the kids' mobile phones which showed just how mad she was. One video – shot in a college room with a slippery, highly polished wooden floor – showed Georgia in her socks being dragged along by four or five lads as though she was water-skiing. Everyone had a little story to tell about her and I went from one person to the next, listening to their tales, as drink after drink was pressed into my hands. There wasn't time to stop and think, or feel sad.

We got home about 11pm – mentally and physically exhausted – and collapsed into bed. At the time, I felt like we'd given Georgia a good send-off, but the reality of what we'd just been through together only kicked in a few days later. Yes, it had all gone smoothly, and there had even been lighter moments of laughter among the tears as we'd remembered the happier times. But really, it had been like working to a schedule, all laid out for us. To some extent we'd lost control – we hadn't had a normal funeral where you can have a proper cry, let everything out and then reminisce with close friends and family. It had been a whirlwind. We'd gone through the motions, but saying goodbye to Georgia had escalated into a show funeral.

Over the last few weeks, we'd endured blow after blow: Georgia going missing, the fruitless search, the realisation that she was dead, and finally saying goodbye. Now, each day brought fresh revelations – always bad news – from the police. They were learning more and more about what Jamie had got away with in the past, and about how he'd murdered Georgia. Revelations of possible police failures sent us straight into digging mode, and we see-sawed back and forth between shock and anger. About ten days after the funeral, Tony Skelding called round. The police wanted to share more information about what had happened to Georgia, and suggested meeting at one of the quieter police stations. Perhaps they thought a more informal setting would make it easier on us, but really, nothing could have softened the blow.

For most people, a funeral means the close of a chapter and the start of the long process of healing. But for us, the nightmare was only just beginning.

NINE

A car picked Steve and I up, and drove us the 20 miles to Wem, a little market town just north of Shrewsbury. The police station was a long, red brick building with Velux windows studding the roof. We went in through a side door and straight into a conference room where six or seven police officers were gathered around a long table. Among them were Tonks, McGee and Paul Hopwood – one of the sergeants from Steve's work.

Tonks began by explaining in medical terms how Georgia had died: from pressure to her neck – which we knew had been caused by the rope – resulting in asphyxiation. It wasn't something I needed to hear again, and at first I wondered if this was just a formality.

But they had much more to say.

The mood was solemn and serious, and it was clear to me these hardened officers were struggling to find the words to tell us what they knew. As Tonks went on, the conversation became more and more technical. The forensic terminology was bewildering. *I haven't got a clue what you're on about*, I thought. No doubt Steve was taking it all in, because it was familiar territory for him, but I sat there for a while looking dumbfounded before deciding I couldn't take any more.

"I'm really sorry," I said. "I'm sure Steve knows what you're talking about but it's all jargon to me."

Tonks nodded with understanding. Perhaps he'd forgotten there was a civilian in the room – me.

"Of course. Sorry Lynnette. We're going to move on in any case…"

From there, without warning, the conversation suddenly turned pitch black. Tonks' words – with interjections from Paul Hopwood – carved images in my mind which twisted deep and left me reeling with shock. We already had a good idea of how Georgia had died, but now it was described in excruciating detail, along with the lengths Jamie had gone to in planning and carrying out her murder.

In preparation, he'd looped the rope over an oar wedged across the loft hatch on his landing. He'd bought high heels, a leather jacket and shorts for Georgia to wear, and he'd told her in a text message the photo shoot would be a 'simulation hanging'.

You'd be standing on a box, I'd edit that (the box) out on a computer to make it look like you're floating, are you OK with that?

There'd been no reply from Georgia. In previous texts, he'd pestered and pestered her to take part in the shoot. She'd told him no less than nine times that she wasn't interested. In the end, he'd worn her down with emotional blackmail: *Don't let me down. I'm in a rut. I need this.*

It was pure agony to hear, but – if you can believe it – what came next was even worse, as we were told what Jamie had done to Georgia after killing her. It was information no mother or father should ever have to hear, and as I listened with mounting horror, I wished with all my heart that I'd sat this meeting out. Having heard it, I'd never be able to forget. Jamie's cruelty was on another level, he was even more demented and twisted than we'd imagined.

After photographing Georgia's dying moments, Jamie had stripped her naked and posed her body in various rooms around the house, recording it all on his camera. The police didn't hold back on any of the sordid details, and as they told me how Jamie had abused Georgia, I burst into tears. I can't say he had sex with her, because of course she wasn't able to give her consent. He'd raped her dead body over and over again. It was horrendous. Not for the first time, I felt physically sick. As one of the officers began detailing where on Georgia they'd found Jamie's semen, I held my hands up.

"This is too much," I sobbed. "We're going to have to take a break."

Steve felt the same. In fact, everyone did. The tension was unbearable. We slipped out to the car park, where we stood trembling in the bright summer sunshine, as though we were immune to its warmth and overcome with shivers. Away over the other side, the officers huddled, feet shuffling on the tarmac, heads bowed. It was agony for them, too.

"I don't think I can do this," I said. Of course, the police hadn't set out to hurt us deliberately. It was well-meaning, in a way: Jamie's crime was so extreme, they knew the media were going to have a field day, and they didn't want us hearing this awful detail from the papers or in court. If it had to come from anyone, it was coming from them.

After 20 minutes or so, we reluctantly went back inside, where the onslaught continued. Maybe they thought that, as a police officer, Steve was used to it, that he could take it. But the reality was, he couldn't. They were recounting the most painful, intimate details of his own daughter's murder, while I sat right beside him. Yes, I knew about the cases Steve worked on, but my knowledge rarely went further than what you might read in the local newspaper when a case came to court. He certainly didn't come home and tell me all the gory details over the dinner table. To suddenly be confronted with all this shocking, distressing detail would have shaken anyone, never mind that our own daughter was at the heart of it.

I left the police station feeling lower than ever. I'd arrived already struggling to comprehend the brutality and sheer evil of Georgia's murder, but what I'd learned now had made it even worse. Later than night, I lay awake in the darkness, trapped in a limbo of enraged exhaustion. I was desperate for the release of sleep, but dreaded closing my eyes – because whenever I did, I was tormented with visions of what Jamie had done to Georgia. They'd been seared into my mind. I'd never shake them off.

In the moments when I managed to channel my anger away from despair and towards some clarity, I was already beginning to think about accountability. Tonks and McGee had said the mistakes certain people had made in dealing with Jamie's earlier offences might cost them their jobs. These things often have a habit of being swept under the carpet when no one's looking, but – behind the scenes – questions were already being asked.

Steve Tonks paid a visit, this time with the head of complaints and discipline at West Mercia Police. "We've just come to let you know – it seems Dick Langton had some involvement in dealing with Reynolds' previous offending," he said.

By now, Dick had already set up a charity to look after the surplus cash raised in Georgia's memory. We'd called it the Georgia Williams Trust. There were plans afoot for more fundraising events, building a lasting legacy to Georgia. The aim was to build a pot of cash to benefit local kids, get them involved in outdoor activities.

"How do you mean?" I asked, wondering for a moment what I'd got myself into.

"It's nothing to worry about," Tonks said. "We've checked and he's on the extreme periphery of things. It's fine for him to get involved with the Trust."

"As long as you're sure…"

"Yeah, he's OK."

It was a relief. Dick was proving to be a fine chairman and I was grateful for the effort. I had some input into who the other trustees should be – Scarlett was on the board, representatives from school, cadets, the college and Telford United. Although at this stage I wasn't in a fit state to get fully involved, it was still a welcome distraction, and it gave Georgia's friends a positive focus. I'd get little notes through from them telling me about the arrangements for the latest fundraiser, or how much they'd raised. It was a way for us to stay in touch. I knew the other trustees were competent, professional people and with Dick at the helm I was sure they'd do a good job. The last thing you want is a charity in your daughter's name being run badly. In no time, they'd organised a charity music festival in Bowring Park featuring a load of local college bands. Steve came up with the name – Ferret Fest – after telling Dick the origin of Georgia's nickname.

"That's a great idea," Dick said.

And it was. Something about the name and the ferret logo captured the kids' imagination.

Steve, however, was picking up an altogether different vibe from Dick. Maybe he was naturally suspicious after years on the job. Perhaps it was police officer's intuition. Or maybe he just knew a bad apple when he saw one.

"I don't know what it is, but I don't trust him," Steve said.

"Oh, come on…" I said.

"I'm telling you. There's something about him."

A week after the first Ferret Fest in September 2013, McFly were playing at a family festival – T Party in Telford. The gig had been organised months before and Georgia had been buzzing about it. Now Dick was arranging for her to be there in name at least after speaking to the organisers.

"They've agreed to let us have a charity stand there!" he told us excitedly.

"Oh, that's great news. Well done!" I said.

"Yeah – and I've managed to nab us really good seats right at the front!" Dick continued.

Steve's face dropped. He couldn't believe how insensitive Langton was being. "I'm not going to any concert. Why the fuck would I want to go to a concert? My daughter's been murdered and she was planning to go!"

Dick shrugged and said: "Oh, OK. Is it alright if I take the kids then?"

Steve was seething. I was in shock. It was totally dismissive of what the charity was all about, what it stood for.

In the moment, Steve let it go. "See?" he said later. "I don't like him."

I must admit, I was a bit more wary after that, but for the time being I pushed those fears to one side. We had enough to worry about.

Jamie Reynolds was yet to appear in Crown Court for the first time, and we were still in a state of shock from the meeting at Wem, when Paul Hopwood turned up at the house with another officer, Chris Henry. I knew their investigation into Jamie was well underway, because officers were forever sending over bits of paperwork for Steve to check in case they'd missed anything.

What do they want him to do now? I thought. Steve needed some peace. We both did. We were still grieving – or trying to – but Steve was being pulled into the investigation.

'Hoppy', as Steve knew him, sat himself down. I steeled myself for more bad news. It was always bad.

"So – as you know we're preparing the case," Hoppy began.

They were going through everything with a fine-tooth comb and wanted to tell us about something they'd found on Jamie's computer.

"Go on," Steve said.

"Well – he had this list of women he wanted to kill," said Hoppy. "Thirty-two of them, and we're just in the process of devising a strategy to tell them."

By now, very little surprised me. But still I gasped at this.

"We don't want them to hear it for the first time in court," Hoppy continued. He paused and said: "And there's something else."

Christ, what now, I thought.

"Two of the girls on this list are friends of Scarlett's."

"What?" I said, incredulous. "Which friends?"

"It's Jadine," Hoppy said, before naming another girl. She's never been identified, so I'm keeping her name out of it. But Jadine wasn't just Scarlett's friend. She was her best friend. I felt sick. The three girls had been close at school. It was as though Jamie had our whole family on his radar, way back then. Any one – or all three – of those girls could have become victims of his sick, devious mind.

We sat in silence for a moment, shaking our heads in disbelief.

But the hits kept coming.

The two girls' friendship with Scarlett wasn't the only reason they needed to tell us about them. They'd also turned up some photos of the girls, which Jamie had doctored.

"Doctored how?" I asked, appalled.

Reynolds had sexualised the photos by colouring the girls' lips bright red. Then he'd drawn nooses around their necks and added bulging eyes. The police felt Jadine and the other girl had at one stage been definite targets for murder, and... it seemed West Mercia had had these photos on file for a while. The other 30 girls were Jamie's 'back-ups'. I held my head in my hands. My mouth hung open, flabbergasted. It was just inconceivable.

"What do you mean they've had them for a while? How long are we talking?" Steve asked.

In fact, West Mercia had them since 2008, but Hoppy and the rest of the MIU team had only been made aware of them in the last few days as they investigated Georgia's murder and reviewed the old file on Jamie.

"Did anyone go and see the girls five years ago?" Steve replied.

Hoppy glanced away, lips clamped tightly shut. His silence spoke volumes.

"I'll take that as a no," Steve said.

Surely if they'd been told, they'd have warned Scarlett, and she'd have warned Georgia. And us. The word on Jamie Reynolds would have spread like wildfire. He'd have been labelled the deviant, dangerous, predator that he was. Girls would have avoided him like the plague. Georgia and her friends would never have dreamt of getting in a car with a weirdo like that. They'd never have gone to the cinema with him, certainly wouldn't have walked him home through the park alone. And would Georgia have trotted off round his house to help with his 'simulation hanging' photos, knowing he'd been cobbling together images of her sister's mates with nooses around their neck? Of course not!

She'd still be alive.

If she'd known, Georgia would still be alive.

I shook my head in disbelief once more. I felt like I could burst.

"What happens now?" Steve asked.

"We'll have to talk to the girls, put some counselling in place for them," Hoppy said.

It was the least they could do.

A couple of weeks passed while we left it to the police to break this awful news to the girls. Hoppy asked that we keep it in the family while they worked out a strategy. We told Scarlett, and she was rightly furious. She'd just lost her sister and now she'd found out Jamie had harboured thoughts of killing her friends as well.

"Who else is on his list?" she fumed. "Am I on it?"

By now, nothing would have surprised me, but apparently she wasn't.

In the months after Georgia's murder, Scarlett could barely face leaving the house except for work. I couldn't even handle that. She'd pop up to Jadine's from time to time, and after Hoppy gave us the nod that the girls on Jamie's kill list had been informed, Scarlett called round to see her. She came home later that night seething. Jadine was furious. And when we heard from the second girl in their friendship trio, she was even angrier still.

In fact, the other girl's mum *had* received a half-cocked warning from her college – years back, in 2008 – to keep her away from Jamie. When she'd asked why, they'd told her that was all she needed to know, and that they couldn't say any more.

"I feel sick," the girl told us. "I'm so sorry." Then she shuddered. "Ugh! You know – he used to come up to me in class and say stuff like, 'why don't you wear your sexy high-heel boots and red lipstick to school'. He was so creepy!"

Jadine couldn't wrap her head around why she hadn't had the same warning as her friend.

"It's like my life is worth less somehow," she ranted. "That's basically what they're saying. How can that be right?"

Out of the blue, the girl who Jamie had attacked back in 2008 got in touch through our family liaison officer. She was eager to meet. I'm going to call her Alice. That's not her real name, but her identity's a secret, and after what happened to her, she's gone to great lengths to keep it that way. I was nervous about meeting because I didn't know what to expect, had no idea what her life was like now or how it had been affected by her encounter with Reynolds. We'd been warned she was reluctant to get involved with the current investigation into Jamie. Her view was: "You weren't interested before. You did nothing. Why come to me now?"

Alice was as confused and unsure about getting together as I was, but after some to and fro over a period of weeks, she'd decided she did want to meet, and she arranged to bring her sister-in-law for support.

We knew what time to expect her, and Steve and I were looking out the window as Alice turned the corner into ours. My pulse quickened and I felt a jolt of shock. *Oh my God!* I thought as Steve and I both did a double take – Alice looked just like an older version of Georgia, how she might have been at the age of 25. She was petite, slim and with the same flame-red hair. It was uncanny, almost eerie.

We invited the two women in and put the kettle on before settling in the front room. I could tell as soon as Alice began talking that she was painfully shy, the most timid person I'd ever met. She sat on the sofa almost folded in on herself, meek and scrunched-up.

"I feel so awful. I just wanted to give you my condolences," Alice said, her voice breaking. She was a swirl of emotions, the expression on her face shifting from anger to deep sorrow.

"Thank you," I said. "It's good of you to come round." I could see how hard this was for her, her knuckles standing out white as she gripped her mug.

"I knew straight away, as soon as I saw on the news about Georgia going missing, I said to myself, 'That's Reynolds.'" Alice glanced over at the framed photo of Georgia on the mantelpiece. The uncanny similarity obviously wasn't lost on her. "I saw her picture on the TV. I couldn't believe how much she looked like me."

Alice explained how she'd met Jamie at New College. Like us, she lived only a short distance from his parents' house on Avondale Road, and the pair of them would walk home together at the end of classes. They were just friends, a couple of kids who lived locally who happened to find themselves on the same college course.

"We were walking back one evening and Jamie said he had this project to do, it had to be in next week and he needed some help," said Alice. "It was something on a book, but he wanted to do it in photo form."

My heart stopped. I wanted to say something, but I bit my tongue. This was five years before Georgia's murder, in January 2008. Five years – and Jamie had spun an almost identical story, playing on the kindness and generosity of his victim. I wanted to hear every word Alice had to say, so instead of intervening, I let her continue her story between halting sobs.

Jamie asked her to come to the house, a brick-built semi-detached with bay windows top and bottom, and an extension built out over the garage. Just like Georgia, she was happy to help, and did just as Jamie asked. Jamie invited her in and motioned for her to go upstairs to his room.

"It's fine," she told him, staying put in the hallway. "I'm OK here."

"Or go through to the living room?" Jamie suggested, disappearing into the kitchen. "I'll be there in a minute."

"I'll wait here for you," she called after him.

The next second, without warning, Jamie stormed out of the kitchen and clamped his hands around Alice's neck. She tried desperately to fight back, but Jamie was choking the life out of her, and as she struggled for breath, he overpowered her and forced her to the floor. Somehow, Alice managed to wriggle out of Jamie's grip and staggered to her feet – but Jamie pounced again, pinning her to the staircase. Scrabbling frantically, one hand found a bannister rail, and Alice pulled against it to drag herself away from him. She heard the wood crack and splinter but got free of Jamie's grasp and made a dive for the front door. Jamie pressed her up against the wall, but in a final bid for freedom – and in a move that almost certainly saved her life – Alice got the door open, fell through it and ran home as fast as her legs could carry her.

"What did you do?" I said. My heart went out to her. She'd never got over this. "You must have been terrified."

Alice shuddered as she explained how her mum had been away on holiday at the time, so she was all alone in the house. "I was thinking, 'what if he comes for me?'" she said. "I called Mum, she told me to call my uncle, and he called the police."

Alice said a female police officer arrived about an hour later, took a statement from Alice and then left to arrest Jamie.

"Hang on – did anyone from forensics come and see you? Did they take any photos?" Steve asked. It was standard practice for officers to follow-up and return, say, a day later when bruises start to show, so they can gather photo evidence.

Alice broke down. Her sister-in-law wrapped a comforting arm across her shoulders and said: "She never heard from the police again. They just dropped her."

"I couldn't understand it!" Alice blubbed through her tears. "I thought I'd be safe with a female officer handling it – but there was nothing. No one even came back to ask how I was doing."

"Did they do a video interview with you?" Steve asked.

Alice shook her head in reply.

Steve was incredulous. "What about a scenes of crime officer? Surely they sent someone from SOCO round to Jamie's place?"

Alice shrugged. "If they did, no one told me about it."

She went on to explain that after getting home, she'd found a text from Jamie asking her to bring a pair of knee-length boots to the house. She'd been so badly hurt that she almost lost her voice, and the next day she croaked an explanation of Jamie's attack to the pastoral staff at college, while nursing a neck covered in angry bruises.

"I think they assumed the police were dealing with it," she said.

There was a bit of relief for her when Jamie vanished from the college campus for a few days – but Alice's life began to unravel when he returned less than two weeks later, brazenly strutting around as though nothing had happened.

"Unless the police put conditions on him, the college couldn't stop him," she said in disbelief. I think talking to us was the first time she'd had someone to complain to properly who would actually listen to her. "I was just told to steer clear of him! That's all very well, but he lived just around the corner from me and went to the same college! How was I supposed to steer clear of him?"

Apparently, they weren't allowed to interfere with Jamie's human right to an education. *Human rights!* Georgia dead, one girl's life ruined, another 32 on Jamie's kill list, and everyone was fretting about *his* human rights. It was insane!

For all Alice knew, Jamie had got off scot free. She insisted no one else had told her otherwise. Certainly there was no court case, and Jamie continued his life as normal. Emboldened by the complete lack of repercussions, he taunted Alice in college, until she abandoned her plans and dropped out. The future she'd envisioned for herself crumbled before her eyes. With no college qualifications, her dream of going on to university fell apart. Instead, she got a little job nearby and cracked on, keeping her head down and suffering in silence. Jamie even managed to ruin that for her. He found out where she was working, and took pleasure in driving past, winding down the window to shout 'slag' at her. It was too much. In the end, she moved away altogether, even changing her name.

Maybe she was wondering whether she should have pushed harder, that if she'd somehow forced them to listen, everyone would have known what Jamie had done to her. "No one took me seriously. He attacked me, but no one would listen. I felt completely let down," she said.

But we didn't for a second blame her. She was a young, defenceless woman. Any blame lay with Jamie and with the police, for the way they'd dealt with him. Or, rather, *hadn't* dealt with him. The implication was clear: if Jamie had been prosecuted, everyone would have known what he was about. Instead, he'd slipped the net.

As Alice was leaving, I gave her a hug. She'd been so brave sharing her ordeal with us. After we'd said our goodbyes, Scarlett came padding down from her bedroom. "I saw her out the window," she said. "I'm sure I recognise her from school but she wasn't called Alice then."

"She's had to change her name because of Jamie," I said.

He'd stolen her future, her identity, and destroyed her personality. And it looked to us like he'd been let off with little more than a slapped wrist. How many times do we hear the police, charities, and victims themselves say women should be listened to? But if they're not taken seriously, even by female officers, what hope is there?

Meeting Alice had prompted so many questions. The answers were out there somewhere, in police filing cabinets, in officers' pocketbooks, in college records. We owed it to Georgia to find them. If mistakes had been made – mistakes that might cost other women their futures, or even their lives – we had to make sure they were never made again. We had a long road ahead of us.

One question I was certain would never be answered was *why?* Why did Jamie kill Georgia? He was never going to tell us, but I thought I might find some meaning in the expression on his face. Jamie had a court hearing coming up, and I wanted to look that boy in the eye.

TEN

I hunkered over my cup of tea as I heard Steve padding down the stairs. For the first time in weeks, the house was silent. We'd been getting up each day to a relentless drip-feed of information about the investigation into Jamie. There was never enough time for the latest bit of news to sink in before we were hit with something else, never enough time for Steve to be a grieving dad instead of a police detective. He walked into the living room and looked around, confused. Usually, his police colleagues would have been perched on the sofa.

"Where is everyone?" he said.

I shrugged. "It's just us."

Steve sat down beside me and we looked at each other, shell-shocked. "What do we do now?" Steve said.

I was at a loss. "I don't know," I said, shaking my head. We were stuck in a dreadful limbo – Georgia dead, Jamie awaiting his reckoning in court.

For the next few days, we rattled around the house. It was only now, in the silence, that the disaster which had befallen Georgia and our family began to properly sink in. Steve was experiencing a murder inquiry from an entirely new and horrifying perspective. Once an investigation was up and running, he usually had little contact with victims' relatives. Now we found ourselves in their position. For weeks I'd longed for some peace and quiet, some time away from the onslaught to reflect. Now I felt abandoned. It was all or nothing. So when Tony Skelding called round, it caught us by surprise.

"Just checking in," he said. "I wanted to see how you were getting on."

"We're all alone," Steve told him. "We don't know what to do."

"Haven't you heard from the Homicide Service? They should have set you up with a bereavement counsellor by now."

"We haven't heard from anyone."

Tony sighed. It was another oversight. Once again, Steve had been treated as a police officer first, the father of a murder victim second. The police had forgotten to put us forward for counselling. "They should have been in touch ages ago!" Tony said. "Leave it with me, I'll chase it up."

A few weeks later, a woman called Sarah got in touch and came to the house. She was slim, with dark hair and came across as sweet and caring. She'd worked as a prison nurse, but in this new role she'd be giving us some informal counselling. More than anything, she was someone other than police officers we could chat to.

I explained I was relying on sleeping tablets to get any rest.

"Try these," Sarah said, handing me a pack of meditation tapes. "Listen at bedtime, they should help you relax."

"I'll give it a go," I said. I was sceptical, but I was so desperate I was willing to try anything. That night I lay in bed and put the first tape on. The gentle sound of waves lapping against a pebbled beach washed over me. Then a voice began: "Lie back, listen to the ocean…"

I stuck it out for ten minutes before admitting defeat. *I don't feel any different at all!* I thought. *Load of arty farty rubbish!* Maybe it worked for some people, but not for me.

The next day, Steve asked: "Were those tapes any good?"

"What a load of crap! They just annoyed me more than anything," I said.

Then, a few days later, Sarah came round for her weekly scheduled visit.

"How did you get on?" She smiled.

Perhaps feeling so tired had given me a case of verbal diarrhoea, because I didn't hold back. Perhaps after everything that had happened in recent weeks, I was just past caring.

"I'm not going to lie – I thought it was rubbish," I said.

"Oh, I'm sorry to hear that," Sarah replied.

"Yeah – and that woman they've chosen to do the voice-over, she really got on my nerves, didn't she, Steve?"

Steve nodded as I caught Sarah's cheeks flushing crimson.

"Where on earth did they get her from?" I said, pressing on. "That accent! Oh, it just grated on me!"

Then Sarah said: "It's me."

I wanted the ground to swallow me up. What could I say? There was no taking it back, *Oh, now I know it's you I realise it's not so bad after all! I'll give it another go!*

Poor Sarah. She was a nice person, to be fair, and well-meaning, but we both got the feeling she was just going through the motions, working through a tick sheet. After a few more visits she told us: "I've got to take you through what we call the withdrawal phase, so I won't be seeing you as often. But if it's OK with you I'm going to put you in touch with someone I think might be able to help. A guy called Frank Mullane."

After that, the visits petered out. I still lay awake each night, tormented by Georgia's dying moments, and what came after. I still felt angry – all the time. Angry that Georgia had been murdered, angry about what Jamie had done before, angry that the police had messed up. I wanted to scream at them: *Bloody do a proper job!*

Sometimes it boiled over into snapping at Steve. It came across as insensitivity, but really I was screaming inside with absolute fury. One time, as we pulled into the driveway in the car, he slumped over the wheel and burst into tears.

"I can't take this anymore," he sobbed.

It was so unlike Steve. He'd functioned so highly, and now it was all slipping away from him, from us. "No!" I snapped. "You can pack that in – we're not having that!"

I just wanted him back. I was trying to protect Scarlett, too, and felt like I was fighting to hold our lives together. I've spoken since to other women in similar situations, and they'd felt the same. Like tigresses. We'd already lost so much, I couldn't stand the thought of Jamie Reynolds taking any more from us. I remember later, speaking to another counsellor, and her asking: "Why do you think you're here, and what can I help you with?"

I thought the main reason would have been obvious, but I said to her: "I've read about other couples who lose a child, and they end up divorced. I really don't want to go down that road if I can help it." That's always stayed with me, and so I really fight, even now.

Although the initial flurry of press interest had died down, we still had a few persistent reporters knocking on the door. One in particular would not give up. Now Jamie had been charged, no one could actually print a word about the case – other than what came out in court – until it was dealt with. But I guess some reporters were gathering background information on Jamie to use at the close of the court proceedings. They had their own sources, and news of Jamie's previous offending was leaking out.

Steve opened the door one day to this persistent national newspaper reporter. He offered the usual reassurances: He just wanted to talk. He knew how difficult it was for us. If we could just spare him a few minutes of our time.

"I'm sorry," Steve said. "We're not saying anything until the court case is over."

"I've heard Mr Reynolds has been a very naughty boy," the reporter said.

That was putting it mildly. But Steve wasn't being drawn in. "Tell you what – you come to court and you'll hear it all for yourself," he told him.

The police were making progress in their own investigation into how Jamie had slipped the net all those years before, and Steve, Alice and I were invited to Malinsgate police station to discuss next steps.

In the meantime, Frank Mullane – the guy Sarah had referred us to – got in touch. He ran a charity – the Advocacy After Fatal Domestic Abuse. Frank's sister and her son had been murdered by her husband, and Frank spent years unravelling the catalogue of police failures that led to their deaths. Even though Jamie and Georgia were never together as a couple, the fact they'd been friends meant Georgia's murder fell under his remit. He knew exactly what we were up against.

"You've got a fight on your hands," he told us, after driving all the way from Swindon to meet at our house. "And be prepared for disappointment at the end of it all – you might not get the answers you want. This meeting – I'll come with you if you want."

"Would you really do that?" I said.

"You're going to need all the help you can get. And I've been there before."

We met in a large, bright office, with a row of windows down one wall and a long table set in the middle of the room. It was daunting. Karen Manners, West Mercia Police's Assistant Chief Constable, fidgeted with a folder in front of her. Hoppy gave me a nod as I took a seat. Steve sat to one side of me, with

Frank Mullane between us. Alice was on the other. Steve Tonks was there, too. Karen stood and introduced the woman sat beside her as Julie Masters. "Julie will be conducting a MAPPA Discretionary Serious Case Review," she said.

Julie was short and authoritative, and reassuringly confident. I'd known for a week or so that this meeting was on the horizon. In preparation, I'd asked Steve to explain what 'MAPPA' meant. It stands for Multi-Agency Public Protection Arrangements, and it's the process through which police, local authorities, the probation service, health professionals – anyone involved in managing a dangerous offender – work together to safeguard the public.

Clearly in Jamie's case it had been an abject failure, and now I wondered where exactly those failings lay. I hadn't realised until that point how many different organisations were involved. All my anger had been focused on the police, but now it was becoming clear that Georgia had been let down across the board. The aim of the MAPPA review was to work out how, and by who.

Karen picked up the file with a look of disdain on her face, like she'd just used it to scrape something off the sole of her shoe. "I've never come across an inquiry like this. It's the worst file I've ever seen – it's crap! I'm ashamed it's come from our force." Her eyes brimmed with tears as she tossed the folder to the table in disgust. It was pitifully slim.

Is that really it? I thought. *That's all the evidence they gathered on Jamie attacking Alice?* I'd seen more paperwork in a bit of junk mail for selling life insurance.

Regaining her composure, Karen took a seat. "At some point we'll need statements from you, Lynnette. And from you, Alice."

I nodded. "How in depth will it be? Any idea how long it's going to take?"

"I won't beat about the bush, we've got a lot to look at, so it's hard to put a time scale on it. Let me explain…"

Alice wasn't Jamie's only previous victim. There'd been at least one more. It had been a couple of weeks after the attack on Alice that Jamie's stepdad found the doctored images under his bed – Scarlett's friends, with nooses superimposed around their necks. He'd handed them over to the police, along with a cache of indecent pictures from porn sites. Yet somehow, even though there was an obvious sexual motive behind his attack, Jamie was let off with a warning.

It was a warning he completely ignored. Three years later he was pestering a girl from work to go out with him. Another redhead. When she told him she wasn't interested, he rammed his car into hers.

"Well, what did the police do?" Steve asked.

"That's one of the things Julie will be looking at," Karen replied. "She'll be scrutinising every organisation that had contact with Jamie Reynolds, and we'll establish from there where the failings lie," Karen explained. "I can assure you."

Having Frank as back-up, and knowing he had our corner, was a massive comfort. I remember him pulling Karen Manners up on a couple of points, and it turned out he actually knew Julie Masters from a previous case. There would be no wool pulled over Frank's eyes.

Meanwhile, Steve simmered. I could sense the anger boiling off him. "This inquiry had better be thorough, because I'll be scrutinising it," he said, index finger jabbing the table top. "If it's lacking in any way, you'll be hearing from me – and I'll be making it public."

He was reading them the riot act, but I think everyone in that room was on the same page – that first investigation involving Jamie had been a travesty. I came away thinking that if someone – or multiple people – hadn't done a proper job, it was just a matter of time before they were found out. Karen Manners, to give her her due, seemed determined to get to the bottom of it. Whether anyone would be disciplined as a result remained to be seen.

"You did right there," Frank told Steve as we left the station together. "They know exactly what your expectations are – no stone left unturned."

Tony Skelding had been a lifeline for us over those first few weeks and months, helping organise the funeral, flowers, Georgia's death certificate. He'd even sorted out cancelling a forthcoming family holiday and arranging a refund. Georgia had been buzzing for this trip, and in the weeks before she was murdered, she'd put together a family playlist on her phone. On family holidays, we liked to sit out on the patio or balcony together soaking up the sun and listening to the kids' music.

"That phone will be full of memories," I said to Steve. It was a white Samsung with little charms hanging off it. It would have been a treasure trove of photos, video clips and music. But along with Georgia's clothes, jewellery and a pink, spotted satchel, it was still missing. Only one person on the planet could possibly know where these things were, and he was playing dumb – sat in his prison cell, waiting for the court hearing. Jamie Reynolds was taunting us.

"I'll ask Hoppy," Steve said. "See if he can get any more out of him."

Georgia didn't have much in the way of jewellery, but what little she did have, she always cherished. The last time we saw her, she was wearing simple stud earrings. She'd not long since had her nose pierced – we'd kind of discussed it and then one day a tiny, jewelled stud appeared out of the blue. That was missing, too, along with a necklace, a ring she'd had for years, and a watch we'd bought so she could keep track of time at college. None of these things had any real value, but they meant a lot to us. They were part of Georgia, and we wanted them back. The police had quizzed Jamie about what he'd done with them, but he was vague and evasive at best.

"It's the same story," Hoppy told us after one visit. "He says he dumped a bin bag in a waste skip at some services near Preston, and another one somewhere else. He can't remember where."

I fumed. He was still trying to hurt us, control us.

Now Hoppy arranged a prison visit with Jamie for another try, reporting back a few days later.

"He's sticking to this story about Preston. But we asked him again about the rest and we might have a lead. It's a bit vague…"

"Go on," said Steve.

"He said he remembers driving down a stretch of road, there was a patch of gravel at the side, and he threw a black bin bag into a field. It's not much to go on, but we know where the road is. We'll check it out."

"Thank you!" I said. It was something to hope for at least. Once again Hoppy had gone out of his way for us. He knew how important these things were to us. And I suppose, in a way, they meant a lot to him as well, because he'd known Georgia, too.

I was on tenterhooks for the next couple of days, before Hoppy and a colleague drove out to this stretch of road in Wales. Later, when he turned up at the house, I hoped against hope he was bringing some positive news.

"We drove up and down, keeping our eyes peeled," he said. "And then a strange thing happened. We were passing this overgrown patch of land and I saw a flash of black polythene just a couple of inches above the grass."

"Oh my God!" I gasped. "You found it!"

"Yes – and no," Hoppy replied. "We pulled over and sure enough it was some of Georgia's stuff. Her clothes."

"No jewellery? Phone?"

"No, sorry Lynnette."

"Can we have them? Her clothes?"

"They're not in a very good condition, I don't think there's even any point us showing you."

Hoppy paused as a dark shadow crossed his face.

"What else?" Steve asked.

The bag also contained the red rope and handcuffs Jamie had used to hang Georgia.

The bastard, I thought. *He's done that deliberately!*

I was convinced. We knew how calculating Jamie could be. He'd split Georgia's possessions up. The more personal things – the items we really wanted back because they meant something to us – were still missing. He'd probably hidden them somewhere, hoping one day he'd return to recover them so he could keep them as trophies, a grim reminder of his awful crime. Instead he'd led us to a bag of mouldy clothes – plus the rope and handcuffs he'd used to kill our daughter. Things we'd never want to see in a million years. *He knows exactly what he's doing*, I thought. *He's got one over on us again.*

Setbacks like this kept me wide awake at night, tossing and turning, burning with anger in the darkness. The lack of sleep meant I'd wake each morning even less able to cope with the day ahead, and so on. It was a vicious circle.

A blessing came in the guise of Maxine returning to our troubled household. She'd kept in touch while she was being fostered elsewhere, but she'd struggled to settle. My heart ached reading messages from her.

"Would you consider taking her back?" one of the social workers asked one day. "Do you think you're ready?"

I was unsure, but we discussed it together as a family and decided it was what Georgia would have wanted.

"Let's give it a try," I told the social worker. "If it doesn't work out for us, or for her, we'll have to call it a day – but we'll see."

In fact, Maxine slotted straight back in, and having her around actually helped. Fostering gave me focus. There were meetings or training sessions to attend, paperwork to complete. I had a reason to get up in the morning to ferry Maxine to school.

On the way home, I began stopping off at Avondale Road and sitting outside Jamie's house in the car. Questions swirled around my head. Not least – *why?* As I sat and stared at the house, I envisioned smoke curling from cracked windows and dancing flames licking the guttering. I hated it. To me, it was pure evil, written in bricks and wood and glass. I wanted it gone, reduced to smouldering ashes. If it had been a detached property, I'd have probably burned it down myself.

September 2013 would have marked Georgia's 18th birthday – a milestone she'd been so looking forward to. Never in a million years did I imagine we'd be remembering it in the way that we did. Leaving a card for her in her empty bedroom. Buying her a wine glass with 18 on it that would sit, untouched by her lips, on her dresser. Placing a pot plant on the bench in Bowring Park among the champagne bottles and friendship bracelets left by her mates. Instead of hosting a party or joining Georgia for her first legal drink in the Haygate pub, we opened our doors to groups of her friends who sat swapping memories in her bedroom. It was a comfort, but seeing them growing up, moving on and realising their dreams could be gutting. I remember one message among the thousands I got on Facebook – *Who knows where you'd have been now Georgia, where you'd have been flying? We never thought you'd be flying where you are.* It was so true. All those moments and achievements that her friends got to experience – university, jobs, weddings, babies – had been taken from her.

A few weeks later, Jamie was due to appear at Birmingham Crown Court. That morning is a blur to me. I can't remember eating and I dressed thinking only of Georgia. *Got to be smart,* I told myself. *We're representing her.*

A police car picked us up, drove us to Birmingham, and pulled into the back of the court – perhaps in an effort to avoid the press. Inevitably a few had arrived there before us. Photographers jostled to get the best shot, cameras bristling. I set my best poker face against their lenses. There was nothing to smile about, but I didn't want my hurt splashed all over the newspapers either. With Scarlett at my elbow, I looked straight ahead and marched towards the door.

I was full of trepidation. I'd never been in a court before, and while it was an environment Steve felt quite at home in, I found it scary and bewildering. After pushing through the door, a security guard had us empty our pockets into a tray. I handed my bag over for inspection and walked through the arch of the metal detector feeling slightly lost, anxious and self-conscious. Once more, I was in a situation I'd never expected life to take me: at Crown Court, waiting to face the man who murdered our daughter.

We were led through a foyer with rows of plastic and metal chairs, a place full of despair. I didn't have a clue what was going on, and so just went with the flow, following orders. Go here. Stand there. Sit over there. The police showed us into a room off the foyer and I stood bemused in the midst of a flurry of activity. Barristers, members of the Crown Prosecution Service, and police officers bustled in and out, brandishing files and folders. Everyone was second-guessing what the likely outcome was going to be. The whole thing felt like a big game, a circus. The gowns and wigs added to the theatricality. We were backstage, waiting for the grim show to begin.

One of the barristers walked in and explained he'd had the nod from defence that there might be some kind of delay.

"We'll have to sit tight," he said. "They're still speaking to their client, but it'll come out in court. We'll just have to wait and see what happens."

The knot in my tummy tightened. It felt like Jamie was still calling all the shots, dictating how things were going to pan out. Then, finally, they were ready for us. We filed into court and took seats in the benches reserved for family members. The press was stationed in a row opposite. A hush fell as two security guards appeared in the dock, between them a clean-cut young man wearing glasses, and dressed smartly in a dark suit. *Who's this?* I thought, wondering for a moment if we'd been called in early by mistake. It took a second to register and I did a double take – the smart young man was Jamie Reynolds. He'd had his hair cut short and his beard was now trimmed into a neat goatee. Some of the chubbiness had fallen away from his cheeks.

"You'd hardly believe it's the same bloke!" I said to Scarlett out of the corner of my mouth. He looked almost respectable, as though butter wouldn't melt. *You're not fooling me*, I thought. *Doesn't matter how smart you look, I know what you did.*

There was some legal to and fro and I couldn't help thinking again how much like a theatre it was. Everyone spoke using pompous words, and the two barristers seemed to be sparring with each other. It was just a show of one-upmanship, a game. At the centre of it all was our grief, and Georgia's murder. I couldn't help feeling like that had been lost somewhere along the way.

The court clerk asked Jamie to stand and confirm his name.

"Jamie Reynolds," he replied.

"You are charged on this indictment with murder. Do you plead guilty or not guilty?"

"Not guilty," Jamie said.

Unbelievable, I thought. The arrogance of him! He'd photographed Georgia as she died at his hands. The evidence was overwhelming. *How on earth does he think he's getting out of this?*

A clue came from Jamie's barrister – he wanted more time for another psychological assessment. There'd already been two. Jamie's own defence team had commissioned one report, and it seemed now they were scrabbling to find grounds for a 'diminished responsibility' defence – that Jamie was mentally ill when he'd killed Georgia. The problem was, a psychiatrist acting for the prosecution had already decided Jamie showed no signs of mental illness.

I glared at Jamie, willing him to look at me, as I clung to Scarlett's hand. I wanted him to see the hate written large on my face, to read in my expression how much I wanted to kill him. Tears ran down my cheeks. The effort of staring at Jamie was all that stopped me from breaking down. I know some people in our position have found it in themselves to forgive – but not me. Not ever, and I don't care who knows it. But Jamie didn't even have the courage to look up – instead he sat with his head bowed while the judge expressed his frustration with the delay. As I tried to focus on what was being said – while beaming my hate across the courtroom to the dock – the reporters opposite scribbled notes in shorthand. Instead of looking at the judge and barristers, their gaze seemed to fall on us. I shifted in my seat, uncomfortable once again with the unwanted attention, in our private loss being played out in public.

"Look at him," Scarlett seethed. "He hasn't even got the balls to look over."

Jamie was trying to drag things out, prolong our torment. The case was going to trial, and the judge set a date for two months' time – December 2nd. After days of worry in the build-up to this court case, getting ourselves hyped up to go, it was all over in about half an hour. I walked back to the car feeling deflated. Jamie Reynolds was calling the shots.

ELEVEN

I pushed my trolley around Morrisons in a daze. Other than dropping Maxine off at school, I rarely went out unless I really had to. The High Street was off limits for months, years even. Every corner sparked a memory that cut to the quick. Meeting the two girls after work. Cafe stops for snacks and coffee. Shopping trips. Happy times when our family had been complete, when we had no inkling of what was coming.

But we had to eat. So I went through the motions, dragging myself around the supermarket, my senses fuzzy around the edges, colours faded, sound muffled – as though underwater. Gripping the cold plastic handle of the trolley, I battled to keep my emotions trembling below the surface. I was never far from tears, and it didn't take much to set them off. Eyes scanning the chill cabinet, my gaze fell on a fish pie ready meal. Georgia's favourite. A heaving sob bubbled up from somewhere deep and broke through. I moved on, leaning on the trolley for support, tears streaming down my cheeks. Concerned faces swam towards me – looking, staring, and looking away again. Not knowing what to say or do.

Moments like this were forever catching me out. A song on the radio could reduce me to sobs in seconds – Passenger's 'Let Her Go', in particular. In rare moments, I'd clean forget Georgia was gone at all. *Oh, she'll be home in a minute,* I'd think. And then it would hit me like a sledgehammer.

No she won't. Not today. Not ever.

Making tea, it was too easy to forget and get four plates out. Steve and I would even cook for four by mistake. The missing space at the dinner table was another reminder of how off-kilter we were. In the supermarket, I'd pick up four jacket spuds instead of three, and then have to put one back, and then I'd be crying again.

But I had to be strong, because our family was falling apart at the seams, as though Georgia had been the thread that held us all together.

Mum and Dad were struggling too – still are – and like us had retreated into their home, rarely venturing out and keeping themselves to themselves. The joy Dad had found on the terraces of Telford United – with Georgia at his side from the age of seven years old – had been torn to shreds, and for the time being he couldn't even bear to watch a match. Too many painful memories. The fans remembered Georgia in their own way, launching into applause at 17 minutes into every game, signifying her age when she'd been killed. Up in the stands, a banner rippled featuring Georgia's photo and the words 'One of Our Own'.

I feared for Scarlett. She was still young herself, just 22. She was fresh out of uni and just starting out in life, but her frayed emotions meant even little things got on top of her. At work, she'd been moved from a public-facing role to doing the books in the back office. She really needed the distraction of a busy front desk, so being tucked away out back was the worst thing for her. Sometimes, it all got too much and her friends would find her broken and sobbing on the fire escape.

Steve was still off work and he'd been trying to get stuck into a bit of DIY to take his mind off things. Keeping on top of the garden had slipped way down our list of priorities, but we couldn't put it off forever. One day we were both out front, Steve tackling the overgrown hedges, when I popped inside to answer the phone. After I'd hung up I noticed the buzz and rattle of the hedge trimmer had died, and when Steve didn't appear, I went back outside to check on him.

For a split second, I froze. Steve was sprawled on the gravel, his skin a deathly grey pallor. For months, I'd been certain that the pain of losing Georgia, and the stress of everything that had followed, was going to finish one of us off. Either Steve – or me – would literally die of a broken heart. I thought this was it. I ran to Steve, and managed to turn him over.

"Steve! Steve! Wake up!" I said, cradling his head in my hands. He was barely breathing. Tears rolled down my cheeks as I fumbled for my phone and dialled 999. "It's my husband," I said, giving them our address. "He's collapsed! I can't wake him up."

"Is he breathing?" the call handler asked.

"Just about," I said. "Please come quickly."

They got an ambulance on the road. The next few minutes were agonising as I begged Steve to wake up. Then, to my relief, his eyes flickered open.

"Thank God," I said. "I thought I'd lost you."

"I don't know what happened," he stammered, barely able to speak.

"Just stay there a minute," I said, as he tried to sit up.

We waited like that on the drive, Steve taking short, shallow breaths as though he couldn't get enough air to his lungs.

"Come on," he said between gasps. "I think I can make it inside."

I helped him into the house and sat beside him on the settee in the front room. "Follow my breathing," I said, and began taking deep, calm breaths. As he tried to keep time with me, we heard the wail of sirens, and then the ambulance showed up. "Here they are," I said, and got up to let the paramedics in.

They exuded calm and professionalism as they checked his heart and worked with Steve to get his breathing under control. The look of mortal terror began to fade from his face and a little bit of colour crept back into his cheeks.

"What do you think's happened, then?" one of them asked, after running through a series of questions to make sure Steve hadn't suffered concussion.

Steve shrugged. "I can't remember a thing," he said. "I don't know what sparked it off. It came from nowhere. But our daughter was murdered recently... Georgia Williams. You might have heard..."

He'd heard. "You've had a panic attack. And I'm not at all surprised given what you've been through."

He left us with some advice on handling attacks if they happened again – slowing down, getting the breathing in order, and blowing into a paper bag if necessary. It had been a huge wake-up call. We needed to find ways to manage the new-found stresses that had seeped into our lives. But in reality, it was impossible. The trial was weeks away, hanging over us like a cloud. We were wracked with worry. There was so much evidence against Jamie, I was sure he'd be found guilty of *something*. The question was: what? And how long would he be locked up for?

For his latest psychiatric assessment, Jamie had been sent to Rampton Secure Hospital in Nottinghamshire, and it came back to us on the grapevine that – in police parlance – he was looking to play the 'mad card' in court.

"It's like a holiday camp!" Steve told me. He'd been before because of work, and he'd witnessed the living conditions with his own eyes. "Games rooms, satellite TV. Yes it's secure – once they're in there, there's no getting out – but they might as well be in a hotel!"

I worried that Jamie might get away with 'manslaughter on the grounds of diminished responsibility' and spend a cushy few years with his feet up in Rampton, or somewhere like it. He was using every trick in the book to try and weasel his way out of punishment. He'd already shown with his past offending how cunning and sly he could be, pulling the wool over the eyes of countless police officers, often managing to flip the situation and turn himself into the victim. He was a dab hand. So I had to wonder – did he have the capacity to manipulate a psychiatrist and convince the court he was insane?

The other big fear was something I'd never considered until now – that in court, 'life' doesn't necessarily mean 'life'. I was under the illusion that a life sentence meant exactly that – spending the rest of your days behind bars.

"I mean, he could get life but only serve 15 years," Steve said.

"Why would he only do 15 years?"

"The judge sets a tariff. We've had cases where they've been done for murder and they're out in eight."

"What's the point in calling it a life sentence if it's nothing like it!" I snorted.

Steve explained how convicted 'lifers' remain on licence for the rest of their days, even after release from prison, so if they offend again they can be sent back to the cells. But in reality, it doesn't mean a bloody thing – licence or no licence, plenty of killers who are let out go on to kill again. And what happened to Georgia was all the proof anyone needed that dangerous offenders can slip the net – with the most tragic consequences.

"So you're saying he could be out in ten years!" Scarlett fumed. "What if I walk down the street one day and he's just there? How am I supposed to react to that? How can we ever feel safe?"

"I know how I'd react to it," I said. "I'd pick up the nearest thing and stab him with it."

The thought of Jamie being let out to start a new life somewhere, maybe even start a little family, filled me with horror. To think he could actually have a life when he'd taken Georgia's away – and ours as well – was chilling. It must be the same for other families in our position, a slow torture building up to the release date, years and years of worry. *Where are they going to go? Will they do it again? Will they come after me?*

"I'll sit outside the prison," I said. "And when he comes out, I'll get him," I said.

Scarlett nodded. "I'll be there with you."

The police told us the prosecution were aiming for what's called a 'whole life' sentence. Which in this case means exactly that: you go to prison and you die behind bars. I knew the chances were slim, because they're only handed down in exceptional cases – April Jones' murder, for example. Still, for the time being I pinned my hopes on a whole life term. My stomach churned at the thought of going to court again. I was dreading it. But I knew I had to be brave. I wanted to see Jamie again just to show him how much I hated him, and if he was going to be locked away for a very long time, I wanted the satisfaction of seeing it happen.

I barely slept the night before the trial. The next morning I was up at the crack of dawn, pacing and fretting as we waited for the police to pick us up for the drive to Stafford Crown Court. I tried to stay calm, tried to ready myself for what was coming, but I was so anxious I felt like I might implode.

"Do you think he'll change his plea? Go guilty?" I asked Steve.

He shrugged. "Your guess is as good as mine. The evidence is overwhelming – but we've all seen what he's like."

Just the idea of stepping inside court again was terrifying, even though I'd done nothing wrong myself. It was the not knowing that scared me – what surprises lay in wait in that courtroom, what new tactic Jamie was going to dream up to wriggle out of it.

And there was another thing.

"I don't think I can sit through a trial," I said. "I don't want to hear all the details of what happened to her. I couldn't handle it."

I had a certain level of knowledge, and I could barely cope with what I knew. There were some things I wasn't privy to, that I don't ever want to know. For example, I didn't realise it at the time but Hoppy quietly approached Steve during the investigation and had him identify the photos Jamie had taken of Georgia after killing her. The police couldn't just accept as a foregone conclusion that the flame-haired girl in those pictures was her. They had to pin it down, otherwise Jamie could come up with an excuse. *Oh no, you've got it wrong. That's not Georgia, that's something I downloaded off a website.* Someone from the family had to look at those images and say, "Yes – that's Georgia." That awful burden fell to Steve and I know he carries it with him to this day. It's not one I wanted to share, nor did I want those photos aired in the courtroom where Georgia's friends, and the rest of the family, would be exposed to them. They'd never be able to get them out of their heads.

The other big worry was how Jamie's defence might tarnish Georgia's memory. What work of fiction would they come up with to explain why she was at Jamie's in the first place? You hear victims' names dragged through the mud in court all the time with these ridiculous 'rough sex' defences. I couldn't bear the thought of Jamie telling made-up stories about Georgia when she couldn't answer back. Steve had the same fears and had a word with the prosecution barrister for some guidance. To our relief, it didn't look as though the defence were planning to dirty Georgia's name, or suggest she and Jamie were in some kind of relationship. But you never knew what they might pull out of the bag on the day. The mind boggled trying to imagine what outlandish lie Jamie was going to come up with to explain away what he'd done.

Steve, Scarlett and I were a bundle of nerves as Hoppy drove us to Stafford Crown Court.

"He could drag this out for years," I sighed.

"If he goes down the mad route…" Steve said.

"That's what I'm worried about. Meanwhile he'll have his bloody feet up in some holiday camp." I was furious to think he might be working the system, trying to get himself a 'better' life – even if it wasn't the life he really wanted – when in fact he didn't deserve one at all.

Once again the pavement outside the court was mobbed with press – reporters, photographers and guys with bulky TV cameras balanced on their shoulders or on top of tripods. We were whisked into the back entrance, down corridors, and past the judge's chambers. This time, they went to some effort to make the court experience less intimidating for me and Scarlett. A couple of victim support workers – a man and a woman – told us what to expect in court, and we were given a guided tour before the hearing got underway so we'd know exactly where everyone would be sitting. They pointed out the witness box and the dock, where Jamie would sit behind a protective screen of reinforced glass. Although familiarising myself with the court did put me more at ease, it also brought home what an important case this was.

"The jury members sit over there," the man explained, pointing out the jury box. "And once they've been sworn in, the prosecution barrister will outline the facts of the case. After that, we'll begin hearing from the witnesses."

"There's things I don't want to hear…" I said.

"It's been discussed with the judge, and he's agreed to pause proceedings so you can get up and leave."

"Thank you," I said.

As we sat waiting in the police room for the hearing to start, one of the barristers ducked inside the door, closing it softly behind him. Everyone looked at him expectantly.

"We've been advised there is likely to be a change of plea," he said.

Steve, Scarlett and I looked at each other.

"Does that mean…?" I mumbled to Steve.

The barrister nodded. "Just try and stay calm. I'll do the absolute best I can for you."

I wouldn't believe it until I heard the words from Jamie's lips, but it seemed we'd just moved a step closer to Jamie being locked up for good.

We filed in. As we sat waiting, I watched the dock intently for any sign of Jamie appearing from the cells. Reporters were packed elbow to elbow in the press bench, making notes and talking quietly among themselves. Steve, Scarlett and I were sat in the pews on the main floor of the court, with various police officers behind us – Tonks, Hoppy and McGee among them. Matt sat over the other side behind the prosecution solicitors. The balcony above our heads was full of relatives and Georgia's college friends.

Suddenly, the door beside the dock opened a crack, and I caught sight of Jamie, a broad grin on his face. He let go a chuckle as he enjoyed a laugh and joke with one of the barristers, who followed him into the court. Leaving Jamie in the dock, the barrister took his place in front of the judge's bench. While Jamie set his face straight, I screamed inside. *How dare he!* Laughing and joking like he was on some jolly for the day. Dressed in his smart suit and purple tie. Mr Clean Cut. Where was the fear? Where was the remorse? Again, I willed him to look at me. Again, Jamie sat with his head bowed, utterly spineless.

I cast a glance at Matt, who was drilling into Jamie with an equally unwavering, dagger-like stare. Like me and Scarlett, he seemed to be demanding some acknowledgement from Jamie.

The general hubbub in the court settled as the clerk told us to 'all rise' for the judge. He took his seat, and after some preliminary conversation between him and the barristers, the court clerk stood up and said: "Will the defendant please stand?"

Jamie stood, eyes fixed on the ground as the clerk read out the charge. Then I stiffened, squeezing Scarlett's hand, as the clerk asked: "Do you plead guilty or not guilty?"

There was barely time to wonder whether he was really going to do it, because the next thing I heard was a single word coming out of Jamie's mouth: "Guilty."

"Be seated," the clerk told him, as a murmur rippled across the courtroom floor. The reporters in the press bench scribbled notes in their pads. I squeezed Scarlett's hand even tighter as I felt a wave of relief wash over me. *Oh – thank God for that*, I thought.

We'd cleared a huge hurdle, been spared weeks of agony hearing about Georgia's murder in minute detail. It was now inevitable that Jamie would be sent to prison – but for how long? Forever? My pulse quickened as the judge told the court he was considering a whole life term, informing the barristers they should address the question of whether or not Jamie deserved one.

He deserves that and a whole lot more, I thought, recalling the multitudes of people who'd told me Jamie should be hanged for what he'd done, people I'd never have expected to be in support of capital punishment.

The prosecution barrister told the court the evidence included distressing photos of Georgia's death, and suggested only the judge should see them. He went on to talk about the violent, pornographic images which Jamie had corrupted by superimposing the faces of girls he was friends with on Facebook. And he told the court how the police had found – scribbled in Jamie's notepad – horrific sexual fantasies, including one about Georgia. The judge agreed all this material would only be seen by him. It was too awful to be shown or read out in open court. "Some details are of such nature, for them to be given wider publicity would cause untold distress," he said, before adjourning the case for sentence in a couple of weeks' time.

Leaving court, I felt an overwhelming sense of relief. There was an end – of sorts – in sight. We knew now at least that Jamie couldn't drag this out forever, playing the system, manipulating us and the court from the relative comfort of a secure hospital.

Later, the police released a statement on our behalf responding to Jamie's dramatic, last-minute change of plea, which summed up exactly how we felt: "The pain we feel is as raw now as it was when our beautiful daughter was taken from us. We will never, ever be able to make any sense of what happened or why it happened to a young woman as caring, kind and generous as our Georgia.

"Today's guilty plea gives us no satisfaction at all. We do not and will never understand the heartbreaking events of earlier this year that changed our lives forever."

I'd been thinking that if we could get a guilty verdict *and* a whole life sentence, I might reach a point where I could just about cope again. I could blank Jamie out of my mind and never have to worry about him.

My worst fear was that with a standard 'life' sentence of a few years, he'd have something to aim for. We'd be counting down the days until he was released, and when that day arrived, we'd all be out looking for him.

You might think I don't really mean that, but actually – I really do.

The judge had set the date of Jamie's sentencing for December 19th 2013. The question now was – would he send Jamie to prison for the rest of his days?

TWELVE

Seventeen days after Jamie stood in Stafford Crown Court and admitted to killing Georgia, we were back there to witness his punishment. Whatever he had coming to him, I knew it would never be enough. The only fitting penalty for Jamie Reynolds' crime was banned way back in 1965.

Friends and relatives packed the balcony again. Matt took up his position, staring daggers at Jamie, who once more sat motionless in the dock with his head bowed. He'd spent the last couple of weeks in Ashworth high security hospital undergoing yet another psychiatric report. His crime had been so wicked and depraved, perhaps no one could quite believe he was not, in fact, criminally insane.

Please let it be a whole life sentence, I thought as we took a seat. *Just give us that.*

We'd arranged things again so we could quietly leave when the most distressing facts of the case were heard. The prosecution barrister began laying it out for the judge, and the rest of the court. By now, very little was news to us. Jamie's obsession with violent porn stretched back at least 13 years. After his arrest, the police found almost 17,000 depraved images and dozens of pornographic snuff videos stashed on a computer hard drive, as well as more digitally altered photos of girls with ropes added around their necks, or hanging from gibbet irons. Exploring his most nightmarish fantasies, Jamie had put pen to paper, writing short stories about killing women and sexually abusing them. On his phone police found another grim work of fiction he'd titled *Georgia Williams in Surprise*, where he watched her 'dance' as she died at the end of a rope. He'd even written something that read like a script where he described trapping a girl and killing her. It was so uncannily similar to the way he killed Georgia, it might as well have been an instruction manual.

And half this stuff the police knew about bloody years ago! I seethed.

We listened to the texts Jamie had sent Georgia, pestering her to take their friendship somewhere she never wanted it to go.

I want to be with you, you're a stunning young woman.

I enjoy your company, you make me laugh.

I don't know why I'm still interested – damn you 'ginge'.

She tried to let him down gently, even told him she was seeing someone, but he wouldn't take no for an answer. Frustration crept in when he failed to take the hint.

I don't see you in that way. Just stop, I don't want to ruin our friendship. I told you last time, I just want to be friends, Georgia replied.

We heard about Alice, we heard about the girl who spurned Jamie at work and got her car rammed by him in return. She, too, had featured in one of his sick stories and appeared in a doctored image, with a noose around her neck. And we heard of a third victim – yet another redhead – who the police discovered as they worked through Jamie's kill list. He'd invited her to his house in February 2013 – a few months before murdering Georgia – almost certainly planning to kill her. When she tried to leave around midnight, she found the doors locked. She screamed the place down and tried to escape out of a window before Jamie relented and let her go. After she left, Jamie wrote a note to himself: *Remove oar from loft. Cable ties out of drawer.* He bombarded the girl with apologies – and she never reported him. She wouldn't have known Jamie's stash of photos included pictures of her, doctored like the others with added nooses, or that a few weeks later he'd write a story about her, titling it *The Taxi Strangler.*

Jamie had learned well from his mistakes. He'd perfected his techniques and grew ever bolder as the police tiptoed around him. By May 2013, he was ready for what the prosecutor referred to as his "primary target".

Our Georgia.

On that fateful night, lying in wait while Georgia walked to his house, Jamie devoured sadistic pornography.

I'm so excited, please don't be late, he texted her.

He'd prepared everything for what would come next. The oar spanned the loft hatch, red rope dangling below.

And then there were the photos: pictures of Georgia in Jamie's hallway wearing the shorts and leather jacket he'd bought for the 'shoot', and the last one of her alive – taken just after 8pm – with his noose around her neck, smiling obliviously, duped into thinking she was just helping out a pal with his portfolio. I didn't need to hear any more. We knew what happened next. Jamie had snatched up the rope, yanked it tight and watched Georgia die in agony. He'd taken photos of her – and himself – naked all over the house while he abused her body. That was already more detail than I ever wanted to know.

I glared at Jamie. He seemed to have slumped into his seat, arms wrapped around his body as though he was hugging himself.

The judge announced a pause in proceedings and Steve, Scarlett and I filed from court to the lobby outside. When we were out of earshot, the prosecution barrister continued. Still, we heard audible sobs and gasps coming from the public gallery. When one woman let out a piercing cry, Steve remarked: "That's my sister." I felt awful. We'd spared ourselves from the worst, but the rest of the family had to sit there and listen to it all. Right up until that moment in court, Georgia's friends had no real idea of what had happened to her. We hadn't told them. It was hard enough for us to deal with, let alone 17- and 18-year-olds. They were just kids themselves.

One of the court ushers gave us the nod that it was safe to go back in court. Now it was Steve's turn. He'd written a victim impact statement describing the devastation that Georgia's loss had wreaked on our family. Usually, these statements were handed in to the judge, who sometimes read them out in the court when passing sentence. But a recent change in the law meant relatives of victims could read the statements themselves. As far as we knew, Steve was the very first.

He took up position in the witness box and read from his notes:

"Evil took Georgia away from her family and numerous people that loved her. We all lost a truly wonderful person on that evening. We still exist but that's all it is. It's not life anymore. Words are used like 'devastated' and 'crushed', they use them to describe impacts such as this. But there are none yet written that can truly convey to others what it is like, what it is really like to lose your precious daughter. I'm not ashamed to say I cry endlessly from morning to night."

Tears rolled down my own face as I held Scarlett's hand in mine. I glanced over at the press bench and saw reporters pause their note-taking to wipe damp cheeks.

Steve continued.

"We have been damned by evil to endure this sorrow and misery to the end of our natural lives. We miss the sweet smile, the hugs and kisses and her infectious personality. Georgia's life was taken for a few moments of evil self-gratification. The guilty plea didn't stop us having to hear and see things that no parent, in fact no person, should ever have to experience. We have been told about details of the case that are upsetting, horrific and beyond comprehension. Any day when we have to hear evidence of what happened to Georgia leaves us totally and utterly destroyed."

Putting our family's loss into words was an almost impossible task, but Steve had done it perfectly. Half the court was in tears. Everyone was ashen-faced, in shock. Everyone except Jamie Reynolds. Steve had poured his heart out in that witness box, yet there wasn't a flicker of emotion from Jamie.

The judge announced a short break, telling the court: "When we return, we'll hear from the defence." We weren't out long. When we came back in, in recognition of Steve's powerful impact statement, Jamie's defence barrister began by remarking: "How do I follow that?"

I'd been wondering what possible excuse or mitigation he would come up with for a crime as heinous as Jamie's, but it turned out his main goal was to dissuade the judge from handing down that whole life sentence. I listened, my heart thudding, blood pressure spiking, as he argued Jamie was too young to spend the rest of his life inside. At the same time, he was trying to make a big deal out of the fact that Georgia had been a few months away from her 18th birthday. One aggravating factor of Jamie's crime was that – in law – Georgia was still classed a child. But Jamie's barrister seemed to be arguing that, because she was *almost* an adult, that aggravating factor didn't really count. The gall of it. Despite all the hurt he'd inflicted, Jamie was still fighting every inch of the way.

How dare you! I thought. *You were old enough to kill. You've condemned us to a whole life sentence. You're old enough to face the consequences.*

I just couldn't get my head around how a barrister could stand up in court and defend someone like Jamie who was so blatantly guilty. It didn't matter how old Georgia was – Jamie had killed her! I felt like I was watching these two barristers play a game between themselves, one where any sense of fairness and justice had been pushed aside for the sake of sport.

I looked at the judge, Justice Wilkie, hoping his expression might tell me which way he was leaning. But he looked impassive, poker-faced, giving nothing away. This was it. The sentence.

Justice Wilkie began by talking about Georgia and all she'd achieved in the 17 years and nine months she'd had on this Earth. It was a reminder to everyone – if any were needed – of the scale of loss that Jamie's wickedness had caused.

"She was an impressive young woman who brought light and joy into the lives of her family and friends," said the judge. He went on to praise Steve's impact statement, and spoke of our suffering, before saying: "The only sentence I am empowered to pass is one of life imprisonment and I do so. My next task is to consider whether this is a case which calls for a whole life term."

I held my breath and felt Scarlett's hand twitch in mine. *Was he going to do it?* I exhaled, fighting the silent tears brimming my eyes.

The judge continued, describing again Jamie's plot to kill Georgia, and her final hours. "You prepared meticulously for killing her in this way and for getting away with her murder," he said. "Seeing those photographs of her, totally trusting and helpless, unknowing of what you were about to do to her has been almost unbearable."

With his parents away on holiday, and his sister staying with her boyfriend, Jamie had had a small window of opportunity to live out his long-held fantasies, fuelled by years of obsessing over violent pornography. He was absolutely determined to kill. So determined he'd even concocted a back-up plan in case Georgia didn't show up. In the run-up to his parents' departure, he'd messaged sixteen girls, asking them to take part in his photo project. He'd made the shoot – a simulation hanging, as he put it – sound like harmless fun.

Besides Georgia, two other girls agreed to help. Two alternative victims.

With Georgia dead, Jamie had what he wanted. While he took photos of her body, he messaged his two reserves and cancelled the arrangements they'd made to come to his house later the same week. "No doubt for the same purpose," the judge remarked.

The next morning, when Jamie's sister called round to see him, she could have had no idea of the horror that had unfolded in their home – on the landing, in their parents' bedroom, in the living room and in the kitchen – just hours before. She would have been completely oblivious to Georgia lying dead in the back of their stepfather's work van, along with her clothes and jewellery. Jamie behaved perfectly normally. After his sister left – the coast clear again – Jamie packed a sleeping bag and tent and loaded his photos of Georgia onto a hard drive, before setting off for Wrexham.

"You took that with you in the van and it was found when you were arrested. The other items, connected with Georgia, have never been found," Justice Wilkie told Jamie. "The clear implication is that you secreted them with the intention of returning to them, along with the photographic record which you had assembled on the external hard drive, to relive, for your pleasure, the events of that night."

In other words, he hid them to keep as trophies. Maybe they're still in their hiding place to this day. We'll never know.

In Wrexham, Jamie relaxed in a cinema watching a film Georgia had been planning to see with Matt. To the outside world, he was Mr Normal – acting as though nothing had happened. From there, he drove to Nant-y-Garth where he dumped Georgia, then pushed onwards to Glasgow. He went shopping, bought himself a watch, and checked into the Premier Inn. When he was picked up by police, Jamie feigned total memory loss – the same ruse he'd used back in 2008, when he'd claimed he couldn't remember much about attacking Alice.

A psychiatrist, Professor Peckitt, had assessed Jamie over the months he'd spent in prison. "The only narrative that stands up to examination is that you wanted to hang a girl and have sex with her corpse to fulfil a long standing necrophiliac fantasy," said Justice Wilkie, summarising Peckitt's report. "He has expressed the opinion that you are intelligent and plausible, are capable of learning new tactics and strategies, and had the potential to progress to being a serial killer. Whilst you pose an ongoing risk to your own life, you also pose a grave risk to women and will continue to do so for the rest of your life."

Jamie was a serial killer in the making. Hearing that shocked me to the core.

Finally, the judge turned his attention to the sentence. He'd been damning in his appraisal of Jamie's crime. Surely he was going to lock Jamie up forever? I listened with blood rushing in my ears as the judge laid out a number of 'aggravating features' – how Georgia's murder was designed to give 'sadistic and sexual pleasure', how he'd stood there and watched her die when he could have saved her, how he'd violated her body, targeted other women and obsessed over violent porn.

"I have concluded that this is not a marginal or borderline case," explained the judge.

Say it, I willed.

"The sentence I pass is one of life imprisonment. The early release provisions are not to apply to you. I make a whole life order."

There was a gasp around the courtroom. Not a punch-in-the-air 'yes!' More like a slump, a release of tension. From Jamie, there was no reaction. He denied me any eye contact to the end. I poured my hate towards him, towards the back of his head, as he stood and then disappeared from view into the bowels of the court. Gone forever, at least as far as I was concerned.

I felt like I could pass out. I'd wanted the whole life sentence so much, yet still wasn't expecting it. I'd been ready to explode with anger at a standard life sentence, but now I was like a bomb defused.

Back in the police room, everyone was patting each other on the back. For the officers, bless them, it was a huge victory. I know from experience when Steve's returned from a court case, they're on a high after a big result. *Great win today. The judge made the right call. We got justice.*

But now we were both seeing it from the other side. I stood there, feeling awkward and numb. It wasn't a joyous occasion for me. I understood where they were coming from, but regardless of the sentence we'd lost everything. One of the officers must have spotted my dazed look as he came over and said: "Are you OK Lynnette? You seemed really quiet when the judge passed sentence."

"It's just that we don't feel the same way as you," I said. "I think I'm just in shock."

Later, as we were leaving court, one of the reporters came over – the same national newspaper journalist who'd been so persistent months earlier. He looked solemn and apologetic.

"I'm really sorry," he said. "I had no idea what I was dealing with until I heard that."

Friends and family filed out of court, shock and disbelief written all over their faces. Eyes red and puffy, make-up streaked with tears.

"How the hell do I ever trust anyone again?" Scarlett sighed. "You think someone is your friend, and they do that to you."

"I know, love," I said, shaking my head. "I know."

The last six months had been building up to those few hours in court, seeing the back of Jamie's head disappear through a doorway, and watching the door close behind him. Forever. We'd been dropped, screaming, from a great height, and now we'd hit the ground. The sudden release left me with a feeling of nothingness. We'd got the outcome we wanted, and now we had to come to terms with the reality that our lives had been altered forever. There had to be a way through. *What's our life going to be?* I asked myself. *And what do we do now?*

THIRTEEN

I wrestled Georgia's duvet into a fresh cover and spread it on her bed before plumping up her pillow. I'd bought her new sheets, dusted the shelves and vacuumed the floor. The radio screeched jagged guitars and clattering drums. We kept it on day and night – tuned to an indie station – so Georgia had something to listen to. At night, after I'd drawn Georgia's curtains and said goodnight to her, Steve would sit in her room and just talk to her. It was a place of solace for us, but also her friends from air cadets and college. The odd time, they'd phone in advance: "Is it OK if we call round and sit in Georgia's room?" Then I'd hear them chatting away to her as they sat cross-legged on her bed. Or they'd just knock on the door, unannounced, often with a bunch of flowers or some chocolates. "We don't want to intrude…"

I didn't mind at all. Keeping those links with Georgia's mates was a comfort, as though, somehow, she was still close.

I gave Bluey a squeeze as my gaze fell on the trinkets and Disney figurines on Georgia's dresser. They conjured warm memories of Christmases past, moments full of laughter and wonder that we'd never have again. Like the times on Christmas Eve when the children were still little and we'd track Santa's journey across the globe on the North American Aerospace Defense Command website.

"Look, he's on his way, girls! But, unfortunately, I've got to go into work," Steve told them one year, putting on his uniform and making a massive fuss of saying he was off to do a night shift. "By the time I get back, Father Christmas will have brought your presents," he said, kissing them goodbye. "Be good for your mum!"

Steve set off in the car while the girls waved him goodbye at the front door, and after hanging up their stockings and leaving a mince pie out for Santa, they started settling down for bed. It was all a ruse. Instead of clocking in at Malinsgate, Steve was down some country lane changing into a Santa outfit, stuffing a pillow up his top for good measure. When bedtime came, I gave the girls all the usual spiel. "Now – you'll have to be good and make sure you go straight to sleep."

They nodded eagerly.

"But before you get into bed, come to the window and we'll have a quick listen out for Santa's sleigh bells."

Me appearing at the window to close the curtains was Steve's cue to run out from behind a bush in the garden, with a bulging sack of presents slung across his back. When the girls peered out into the darkness, they couldn't believe their eyes. "It's really Father Christmas!" they squealed. "He's real!"

When you've got kids, you wrack your brains coming up with quirky, funny ways to make life exciting and memorable for them. Christmas was one time of year when we really went to town in that respect – not by squandering loads of money, but by spending quality time together with the girls, and making it fun. There was the old, red settee we'd found in an antiques shop, which every Xmas doubled for Santa's sleigh. We set it up with two dining chairs in front, and a Jingle Bells Disney cartoon blasting out of the TV.

"Right – you two in the back," we told the girls.

Steve and I sat in the front and pretended we were going on a sleigh ride, following the cartoon sleigh on the telly. "Hold tight! We're going downhill now!" The girls whooped with glee. "Left turn! Now right!" The kids leaned one way and then the next, howling with laughter.

Steve, Mr Imagination, could turn even the saddest of occasions into something magical. In the run-up to one Christmas, both the girls' two guinea pigs inexplicably died on the same day. We knew they'd be distraught, but Steve came up with an idea.

"I'm going to bury them," he said. "While I'm doing that, see if you can find some glitter."

"Glitter? What for?"

"Go on," he said, "I'll be back in a minute."

Steve found a quiet spot in the garden and laid the guinea pigs to rest. Back in the house he put pen to paper. I peered over his shoulder as he wrote a letter. I gasped – now it all made sense. The girls were going to love it!

"That should do," he said, folding the sheet of paper in three and tucking it into an envelope.

"I'll bring the glitter."

Steve laid the envelope among the straw in the now empty guinea pig hutch, while I sprinkled the floor around it with glitter. Now all we had to do was wait.

It was later that evening when the girls went out to feed their pets, and we followed behind them trying to hide our smiles.

At first they were dismayed to find the guinea pigs had vanished.

"They're gone! They're gone!" they chorused.

Then Scarlett spotted Steve's letter. "It's addressed to Scarlett and Georgia," she said.

"Go on, love, read it," I said.

Georgia let out a gasp as Scarlett read: "Hello girls. This is Santa. Most people don't know this, but baby reindeer start off as guinea pigs – and your two have gone off to become trainee reindeers." Their faces were a picture, full of wonder. We'd spared them the fright of finding two cold, lifeless guinea pigs and instead given them a memory to cherish. That's what it was all about for us.

That was then. But in the wake of Jamie Reynolds' court case it was going to take more than a bit of glitter to raise our spirits. The wonder years sparkle was gone forever, and the tension of the last few weeks had taken its toll. I was exhausted. Apart from buying Maxine a few presents, I'd barely given Christmas a thought. To us, it didn't really exist anymore. It had always been about family, about *both* our children. Now that one was gone, Christmas was something other families did. Where it had once been about fun and celebration, now it was a time for remembrance and reflection.

Thankfully that year, at the suggestion of Sarah, the counsellor, we'd arranged to spend it away from home for the first time ever. With some help from the Moira Foundation, which supports bereaved families, we'd rented a little place down in Devon. The day before Christmas Eve, we packed our suitcases, bringing Bluey along for the ride, and hit the road.

It was a tiny, two up, two down cottage at the end of a narrow, winding lane in the middle of nowhere. A kiss of sea salt in the cool air told us the sea was close by. As we pushed in through the front door, Steve had to stoop to avoid braining himself on the low beams. My eye fell on a little, foot-high white Christmas tree the owner had left – the only decoration. In a way, it summed up perfectly how we felt about Christmas, that it was diminished.

Because the court case had been so intense, I was determined not to dwell on it. I needed to chill. A ten-minute walk down a steep lane led to the beach, and a mile's stroll along the sands brought you to Teignmouth. Watching Scarlett's dog Minnie paddle at the water's edge, with the cold winter wind in my hair, I

187

began to relax into our Not Christmas. Just being around people who didn't know who we were, where our anonymity meant we could blend in, was a blessing.

Maxine thought spending Christmas away was the best thing ever. We'd shielded her from the worst of what had happened to Georgia. She knew the outcome of the court case, but she was fragile herself in her own way and we didn't want to burden her. On Christmas Day, as she tore open her presents, she asked: "Aren't you going to open yours?"

"Oh – we'll get something later," I fibbed.

I cobbled a meal together and we sat around the table to eat. There were no crackers or table decorations, but we layed a place for Georgia, and Bluey sat in her chair. From time to time, she would come up in conversation, but it was still too soon after losing her – and she'd died in such an awful way – that I didn't feel ready to laugh and joke about the childhood years.

After dinner, we hit the beach again. It felt freeing to do something so completely different from our usual routine. On Boxing Day, the sands were full of people in fancy dress, splashing in the waves, blasting away their hangovers. The day after, we went into Exeter and treated Scarlett to a few bits in the sales. Spotting a Little Mermaid figurine, I picked it up and asked her: "What do you think?"

"For Georgia? Yeah – she'd like that."

Just because she was gone, it didn't mean we couldn't buy her things, and we still do it now. When we returned to Telford – back to the real world – that blue mermaid joined the rest of the Disney characters on her dresser.

The real world.

Jamie Reynolds, at least, was out of the picture, but we still had a fight on our hands. We'd just got through the court case, and had had a bit of time to process the verdict, when we were told

West Mercia Police were referring themselves to what was then the Independent Police Complaints Commission. The IPCC for short.

"And so they bloody should do," I said to Steve. There'd been a few hints this was in the pipeline. From the questions we'd been asking – and the non-answers we'd been given – it was obvious the earlier investigations into Jamie stank of laziness. It sounded to us as though there had been a culture of clearing desks rather than proper policing, safeguarding and delivering justice. We both wanted an investigation, but inevitably I could feel the tension and anger cranking back up again. We'd been told people might lose their jobs, and we wanted to see it happen.

Straight off, we were in for a shock. To our utter bemusement, the IPCC turned around and told West Mercia to investigate *themselves*.

"We're not going to get a proper job done if they're telling themselves off, are we!" I complained.

Steve turned to Frank Mullane for advice.

"You've got to keep pushing," said Frank. "Speak to anyone who'll listen. Don't give up."

We tried the MP for Telford and Wrekin, Mark Pritchard. He turned up half an hour late for our meeting and then spent most of the time clock-watching and telling us where he had to be next. He came across as totally clueless, and after he asked us for the umpteenth time what we expected him to do, I stood up and told him: "Actually, we'll go now."

West Mercia were as unhappy with the IPCC decision as we were. They knew if they investigated themselves, we'd be watching. We'd pick them to bits. Over the coming weeks, and then months, they went back to the IPCC time and again. "Look – we really shouldn't be doing this," they told them. "It needs an independent investigation."

But the answer was always the same. The IPCC were too stretched. They didn't have the resources. It wasn't their remit. As though, perhaps, it was too big and complicated for them. No one could really believe the stance they were taking, least of all us.

In the meantime, the Trust was ticking along and I began taking a more active role at the meetings. It was another welcome and much-needed distraction, as well as a way of keeping in touch with people who'd been close to Georgia. At one board meeting at Telford United in early 2014, Dick Langton had an even bigger than usual smile plastered across his face. I knew why. It had filtered through to us that he'd been promoted to Chief Inspector. For the time being, he was on a probationary period, proving he was worthy of the new role over the coming months.

We were all chatting about the various Trust events that had taken place recently and mulling over plans for the rest of the year, when someone mentioned, "Oh – Worfield Golf Club had a fundraiser the other week, apparently it went really well."

Straight away Dick jumped in.

"Yeah, I went into work early so I could get away to the club. I had lunch out there, sat with all the football players from Wolves," he gushed.

We all looked at each other in disbelief. We were all thinking the same thing. *Is that what it's all about?*

At the same time, rumours were coming back to us from police contacts that Dick's promotion hadn't gone down well in the office. It was sticking in people's throats. And mine, if I'm honest. I couldn't help wondering if his work for the Trust had helped him land the new job. I'd never know, because there was no way of finding out, but I was beginning to feel like I'd been used.

As we walked out to the car park after the meeting, Dick had an extra spring in his step. Chest puffed out, he strolled over to a shiny new Jag, with personalised number plates.

"I thought I'd treat myself," Dick said, plipping the car alarm. "You know – for the promotion."

"Right, OK," I said, not sure where to put myself.

"Do you want to sit in it?"

"Err. No – you're alright, Dick. I'm going to get off home."

It was around this time – February 2014 – that Steve began making noises about returning to work. He was in two minds. We both were. It was a double-edged sword – he'd always loved his job, and it's always been in him to work and keep the roof over our heads. Regardless of everything that had happened, there were still bills to pay. But on the flip side, was it really the right kind of job to go back to?

"Plus – I don't know how I'm going to be treated," he said, mulling it over.

The imminent MAPPA review had kicked up some dust at West Mercia, and Steve would be putting himself back in the thick of it, at the centre of the storm. Inevitably, there were going to be occasions when he'd find himself face-to-face with officers who'd messed up.

He talked it through with Hoppy, who was his line manager. They discussed going to other departments, or working in intelligence. Another officer floated the idea of him going back to working in uniform, out of Wellington police station. But none of those options really measured up. Steve wanted to be back among people he knew, in a department he'd been with for years.

"On balance, it's better to be in that camp than out of it," he said. "I can keep an eye on what's going on."

"If you're sure," I said.

"I can keep the pressure up."

West Mercia put a return to work plan in place, and because I'd done some HR and management, they let me give it the once over. To begin with, Steve returned to the Major Investigation Unit at Malinsgate station – just on light duties for a few hours a day, working through boxes and boxes of old coroners' files from his desk. It wasn't the investigative work that he was used to, but it was a start. And it gave him focus.

At first, he'd return home subdued and exhausted. It wasn't the kind of job where you could just sit and watch the clock while you twiddled a pen around your fingers. But West Mercia was genuinely caring and called each day to reassure me that Steve was coping. Soon enough, within the month, he was back at it full time.

However, his return to the office didn't please everyone. He hadn't even been there two weeks when he came home one afternoon absolutely fuming.

"Someone's gone and put a complaint in about me," he said.

"A complaint about what? What are you supposed to have done?"

"Nothing, as far as I know. Seems like someone just doesn't want me there," he shrugged. "Well, I'll be telling them – I'm not budging."

The way Steve's department worked, they had a few offices spread over their region. Steve had done a week at Malinsgate, then moved over to Shrewsbury for a few days. Leaving for home one evening, he was getting in his car when a friendly sergeant came over.

"Word to the wise," he said. "There's a complaint going around from some of the officers in the firing line."

"About me?" Steve asked, dumbfounded.

The sergeant nodded. "They're moaning about you working from Malinsgate."

The next day, with Hoppy in tow, Steve went to see the superintendent for Shropshire, James Tozer. He basically confirmed the complaint. Things were hotting up. Fingers were being pointed. One name in particular had reached Steve's ears – Detective Sergeant Joanne Delahay. For now, he wasn't sure precisely where she fit in West Mercia's previous dealings with Jamie.

"Whoever they are, tell them that if they can't accept responsibility for what they've done, then they shouldn't be police officers," Steve told Tozer. "If they can't shoulder it, tell them they can fuck off. I'll work wherever I want, and wherever I'm needed, just like I always have."

Tozer sighed and asked Steve: "Come on. Where do you want to work? Name your station."

"I've told you – I want to work from here, or Shrewsbury, or wherever I'm required. But these are my two main bases and I'm going nowhere. If anyone needs to choose where they work, if anyone needs to move – it's them.

In other ways, I felt West Mercia had our backs. On the internal investigation, they were still on our side, still forthcoming with information. They wanted an independent inquiry as much as we did, and they suggested we push for it by filing an official complaint against them.

"I'm not allowed to do it while I'm still working there," Steve said. "It'll have to be you, Lynnette."

I sat down with Steve to write the letter, struck by just how bizarre the situation was: I was filing a complaint against Steve's employers over how they'd dealt with a man who'd gone on to murder our daughter. With the hostility Steve was already encountering at work, I had to wonder whether it would just make things worse. But if we wanted an inquiry everyone could stand behind, we had to do it. Frank Mullane agreed. He had connections at the IPCC, but their unwillingness to investigate had left even him scratching his head. "I can't understand it," he told us. After trying and failing to get them to budge, he advised us it was the only way forward.

I wrote that we'd been made aware that previous investigations into Jamie Reynolds had been riddled with mistakes, and that we wanted an independent body to investigate West Mercia Police. It was the only way to guarantee a fair outcome – one both we and the public would have confidence in.

Steve was allowed to have his say, in a roundabout way – he was given permission to add a witness statement of his own. "Using the knowledge that I have gleaned over many years as an investigator, I believe that there are serious shortfalls in the investigation into and the decision making process in the 2008 and 2011 incidents," he wrote. "Although I do not know the full circumstances surrounding each event I feel that I have sufficient information to justify my huge disappointment and personal anger that these travesties have occurred within an organisation that to date I have been proud to serve."

Travesties we both believed had cost Georgia her life. It was a wonder Steve had found the strength to return to work at all.

A few days later, Steve took the letter into the office and filed it. Now, all we could do was wait.

FOURTEEN

Julie Masters handed us a sheaf of papers, secured along one edge with a black strip binder; seventy-two pages in all, printed double-sided.

"I've completed my report, I wanted to give you your copy," Julie said.

We'd been on tenterhooks the last few days. We knew Julie's work on the MAPPA Discretionary Serious Case Review was done, and now she was calling by the house to hand-deliver her findings. "I've been as thorough as I possibly could," she told us. She sounded serious and professional, and I believed her implicitly.

"Thank you," I said, flipping through the report. The name 'Reynolds' – printed in capital letters – leapt out from every page.

"I'll just give you a summary of my findings, then I'll leave you alone to digest them," Julie said.

Julie confirmed the gist of what we'd been hearing from the police for months: their investigation into Jamie's attack on Alice had been bungled from the word go. Steve's view was that – in police parlance – the job was batted away. They wanted it off their desks, done and dusted.

But it didn't end there.

The various agencies involved in managing Jamie afterwards had messed up as well. They either hadn't done their jobs properly, or had failed to share crucial information with each other, or had fallen foul of Jamie's cunning. Any one of these organisations could have called a MAPPA meeting, got everyone together to pool information and make joint decisions. Instead, they'd worked in relative isolation, in what Julie termed 'silos'. With no single department taking the lead for managing Jamie, no one joined the dots, and no firm plan was put in place to protect the people around him. The whole approach had been disjointed and focused on the short term.

No wonder the police want us to keep the report to ourselves, I thought.

I wanted it published, so everyone could read it. But West Mercia had told us that they'd commissioned the report, and so they would decide who got to read it. It was infuriating. It seemed they were determined it would never see the light of day.

"I'll do everything in my power to see this report published," I'd told them. "You're not covering up your mistakes anymore."

Thumbing through the pages, I wondered – *what's the worst they could do?* I could have easily picked up the phone and handed it to the newspapers. But I'd discussed it with Steve, and we'd decided – for now – to bite our tongues and bide our time. We were still pushing for an independent inquiry into West Mercia's role. We desperately needed accountability – both for Georgia, and for the sake of our own sanity. The officers who we believed had failed us had to face the consequences. We'd been told heads were going to roll, so as much as we wanted to tell the world the contents of Julie Masters' seventy-two pages, we couldn't jeopardise what had to come next. Nor did I want to give West Mercia a reason to hold out on us. Thus far, to give them their due, they'd been forthcoming with information.

After Julie left, Steve and I sat down to read the report. It was absolutely damning. As I turned page after page, fuming with anger, I felt a scorching burn in my tummy, and tears of rage sprang from my eyes. It was as bad as we'd feared – and then some.

The investigation into the attack on Alice was full of holes. Jamie's warped obsession with strangulation was literally staring officers in the face. The photos found under his bed and the porn on his computer pointed to a clear sexual motive – but the police used neither to develop their investigation and bring Jamie to court. He'd lured a girl to his home, tried to strangle her, left her in fear of her life – yet was let off with a paltry 'final warning' for common assault. Because he'd been under 18 at the time, legally speaking he was still considered a child.

"Look at this note," I said to Steve, reading about a meeting between Child and Adolescent Mental Health (CAMHS), the police, New College, Adult Social Services and Children's Services. "Whilst Reynolds' potentially harmful offending behaviour is a cause for concern, it is also apparent that he too is vulnerable and that any decisions made could have a profound influence on his future."

Steve blew his cheeks out. "They're more bothered about him than the people around him," he said. "Jamie Reynolds – vulnerable! I've heard it all now."

Jamie's 'final warning' also had implications for how he was supervised in the year or so after the attack. It meant the work he agreed to do to address his offending was actually *voluntary*. No one could force him to attend the sessions. Jamie ducked and dived, gradually withdrawing from contact, while manipulating conversations to distract attention from his offence and to paint himself the victim of a troubled home life. At the same time, Jamie's assurance that he'd left behind his interest in violent porn was taken at face value. No one thought to question it. He even convinced psychiatrists he was sorry for attacking Alice – while behind their backs he was secretly taunting her in college, making her life a misery.

With a likely independent inquiry into West Mercia looming, the MAPPA review didn't go as far as identifying individual officers, or marking them out for discipline. But six other agencies were involved with Jamie after his attack on Alice, and although there were plenty of well-meaning individuals, too often, the left hand didn't know what the right was doing. Nine months after the offence, the only organisation still having any meaningful contact with Jamie was the National Society for the Prevention of Cruelty to Children (NSPCC). They were operating in complete isolation. Their caseworker had no official way of liaising with the police or West Mercia's Youth Offending Service. Jamie picked and chose when he went to sessions, and dictated what they discussed.

"It's just unbelievable," I said to Steve, wiping away tears. "How could they?"

"It just smacks of laziness," Steve said. "Let's go back to the beginning, and read it line by line."

The report confirmed Alice's tearful recollection of the police response to Jamie's attack. She'd fled his house in terror, arriving home in a state of panic and frantically locking doors and windows in case he came after her. Alice's uncle called the police, and a female officer arrived to take a witness statement.

"That's wrong for a start," Steve said. "She should have been interviewed on video."

In the days that followed, no one arranged for photos of Alice's injuries, nor a forensic medical examination. In fact, Alice was all but forgotten. Meanwhile – within hours of trying to strangle her – Jamie touted for sympathy, sending texts pleading forgiveness. He hadn't planned it, he said. He told her he knew he had problems and was undergoing counselling. He said he was sorry, that he'd do something else for his project, asking Alice to keep the incident to herself.

It was all lies. The project didn't exist. And he *had* planned it – because he'd messaged Alice asking her to bring a pair of knee-length, black boots. Jamie told her they were worn by the main character in the book his project was based on – the project he'd fabricated.

Later that evening, January 9th 2008, Jamie was arrested on suspicion of assault. He was rude and evasive, and he continued with the stand-offish attitude in the interview room. As the officer quizzed him, Jamie grew impatient and irritated – not sorry or remorseful. It was all too much for him, he just wanted the matter dealt with. The only real admission she got out of him was that the 'project' had in fact been a ruse – he said he made it up to get Alice round his house so he could 'make friends' with her. In Jamie's version of the attack, he got his hands on Alice's throat once, not three times as she'd claimed, and he helped her out of the house as soon as he came to his senses. No one thought to go back to Alice and run Jamie's story by her.

It was a clever move by Jamie – too clever for West Mercia. Handing them this partial admission gave them enough to treat the attack as a common assault. The MAPPA report said their approach was "narrow" and "aimed at ensuring a speedy resolution".

"Like I said – they just batted it away," Steve seethed.

The photos of Jadine and Scarlett's other friend came to light five days later, when a mental health nurse from the Justice Liaison Service (JLS) visited Jamie's house and met his parents. The JLS intervenes when young people with suspected mental health issues get caught up with the police. Jamie – playing the victim card – told this nurse he hadn't been feeling his usual self in the runup to the attack. He denied using porn and insisted there was no sexual motive – more lies, which were instantly exposed by Jamie's own parents. They gave the nurse the photos of Jadine and her friend, with bulging eyes and nooses drawn around their necks, and told him Jamie had been looking at porn involving women being hanged. Considering the attack on Alice, this new information should have sounded a deafening alarm. Astonishingly, the nurse chose not to tell the police about it.

He *did* however refer Jamie to CAMHS, and a female doctor visited Jamie a few days later, when his stepdad admitted he'd caught him looking at violent pornography as far back as two years previously. The doctor assessed Jamie as posing a "significant risk to others". Later, a colleague advised her the girls in the altered images should be located and warned never to be alone with him. Likewise, the college should be told Jamie was not to be left alone with female students. Information about the pictures should also be passed on to the police, the colleague advised. Rather than going to the police herself, the CAMHS doctor told Jamie's parents to do it.

To their credit, they went the next day. These doctored photos, coupled with the porn, were a golden opportunity for the police. So far, Jamie had offered them no real explanation for attacking Alice – but now they had concrete evidence of his obsession with strangulation and sexual violence. They could have searched his bedroom and poked around his computer. They could have dragged him back in for another interview. They did neither.

"This is where it all goes wrong," Steve said. "They should have taken a statement from his parents, put the photos and pornographic material in as exhibits, and gone for a charge."

If Jamie had been hauled through the courts back in 2008, everyone would have known what he was about. Any work and supervision that followed would have been *compulsory*, ordered by a judge as part of his sentence. His internet use could have been restricted. Alice could have been protected with a restraining order. But no. In Julie Masters' words, the investigation was "blinkered" – the police had made their minds up, they were unwilling to see where this new information might take them. Instead, it was filed away for future reference. That intelligence log might have proved handy if someone had bothered to check it three years later when Jamie struck for a second time, but it was never looked at again.

Meanwhile, the JLS mental health nurse wrote up his report: "Reynolds may have an interest in sexually harmful behaviour and/or violence. The risks Reynolds poses need to be more thoroughly assessed." In fact, he *wanted* Jamie supervised under a multi-agency arrangement, and even said so when he met with a group of representatives from the police, CAMHS, Children's Services and New College. By then, the police were already working towards a reprimand, based on Jamie's young age and lack of criminal record. The only acknowledgement given to Alice at the meeting was that – yes – she and Jamie attended the same college, but apparently there was no reason for their paths to cross. Jamie was back in classes within a couple of weeks of the attack. His rapid return to college was "cause for concern" for Julie. Clearly it was cause for concern for Alice too – because she soon left, and that was the end of her college career.

Regardless of the JLS' fears, no date was set for another multi-agency meeting, and in fact one never took place again – a "serious failing" Julie concluded, adding that Children's Services or the Youth Offending Service (YOS) could have co-ordinated a plan for managing Jamie. But neither did.

It got worse. By now, it had been a month since the attack. Jadine and her friend had been identified in the photos, and representatives from both the girls' colleges met with Children's Services, the JLS and the police. Incredibly, there was debate over whether the girls should be told. The police said no. JLS said no – because it might be too distressing for them. Not only that, they were worried about the "potentially damaging impact of the disclosure on Reynolds".

I shook my head in disbelief. I wanted to shake them by the shoulders and scream: *Why didn't you just blimmin' tell them!* "What's everyone so worried about Jamie Reynolds for?" I yelled. "What about the girls?" Not only Jadine and her friend, but all the other girls Jamie Reynolds came into contact with. Girls like Georgia.

Once more, no thought was given to Alice. The chair of the meeting thought New College had put measures in place to protect her, and hadn't been told she was being terrorised by Jamie. Four weeks in, Alice had been forgotten.

A couple of weeks later, Children's Services met again with the police. CAMHS didn't get an invite and the JLS had withdrawn by now. Jadine and her friend were discussed again, and a social worker pushed for them to be told about the photos. Finally, it was agreed she could contact the girls and determine how well they knew Jamie. But Julie discovered that the meeting with Jadine never took place. The other girl was told to stay away from Jamie, with no explanation why. Julie was scathing about this decision to leave them in the dark, vulnerable and unprotected. "It is difficult to see how they could have helped protect themselves without sufficient information to enable them to do so," she wrote.

While all this was going on, Jamie was seeing mental health workers from CAMHS. He made all the right noises – told them he felt better, his mood had improved, and he was ashamed and embarrassed by the attack on Alice. Problem was, CAMHS had missed those earlier safeguarding meetings, so they had no idea Jamie was making Alice's life hell in college – shoving her, smirking at her in the corridors, calling her a bitch and a slag. CAMHS were left in the dark. Jamie's behaviour outside of the consultation room was the polar opposite to what he told psychiatrists inside it.

"Doesn't really sound like someone who's ashamed and embarrassed, does it?" I scoffed.

"More like someone who's got away with it," Steve agreed.

The YOS, too, were never told about this harassment in college. Two months after Alice complained about him, Jamie was recommended for a final warning, and assessed as 'medium risk'. He agreed to just three months' contact with the YOS, and an extended period of work on his behaviour with the NSPCC. All voluntary. He was meant to be put on the 'Person Posing a Risk to Children' register, but Julie discovered that referral never took place.

Two days later, Children's Services held a final safeguarding meeting and closed the case. Alice's ongoing safety and the wider risk to other girls – including Scarlett's friends – was disregarded, with nothing in place to protect them. Jamie was issued with his final warning shortly after, and the police closed their file.

Over the next three months, Jamie had just five meetings with the YOS. They had no contact with the college and therefore no idea he was harassing Alice. His apparent 'progress' went unchallenged. On his final meeting, Jamie was effectively handed over to the NSPCC to manage, with no plan in place to protect the public.

By now, the charity was the only organisation working with Jamie. CAMHS had all-but withdrawn, and the NSPCC had no formal lines of communication open with anyone else. Jamie must have been thinking, *Why should I bother? What's the worst that could happen?*

The answer, of course, was nothing.

Jamie cancelled his first appointment with his NSPCC caseworker, and skipped the second. He was laughing at them. They tried to press him, but Jamie told them he "wasn't fussed" about meeting. He was already pulling away, and put the whole thing on hold until September, after the summer holidays. Ultimately it was actually December before they got to do any work with him – nearly a year after the attack. In the meantime, CAMHS took him off his medication for depression, and told his parents they should start trusting him more. His last appointment with mental health workers was in October and they closed their file shortly after. Julie found CAMHS were under the impression he'd been referred to the Risk to Children register, and they also thought he was being managed under a MAPPA. Neither were true. "None of the protective factors CAMHS believed to be in place were in place," Julie wrote.

The NSPCC agreed ten to twelve sessions with Jamie, but he called the shots from the outset – he only wanted to do four or five. He did his best to dictate the focus, telling his caseworker he didn't want to be reminded about the offence. They should move on, he said. She tried to keep him on track, and even got Jamie talking about his interest in torture pornography, but he soon clammed up, complaining of a headache. She thought he was insincere, going through the motions. And she was worried – worried about the way he'd planned his attack on Alice, and worried about his interest in violent porn. Overall, she was worried about the risk he posed. Jamie tried to play it all down, even suggesting his own mum was sick of him going to the sessions. But the caseworker persisted – a "robust" treatment plan was needed, she said, passing her concerns on to the YOS, who in turn forwarded her report to the Probation Service. Because Jamie's sessions were voluntary, Probation didn't file the report electronically, and Julie thought it had probably been destroyed after 12 months. If Jamie reoffended, there was no way to link back to it.

By now, Jamie had turned 18. In the eyes of the law, he was an adult, and he told the NSPCC he didn't want details of his sessions shared with his parents. He met with his caseworker another six times over the following 14 months, but repeatedly turned the conversation towards himself – his exam stresses, his lack of income, even how tough he was finding it to get car insurance. He claimed his stepdad was controlling and abusive, but this picture he painted of his home life went unchallenged, and Julie concluded it was "unrealistic". Jamie's last contact with the NSPCC was in January 2010. They closed the case four months later when he failed to respond to them.

He lay low and got on with his life, working at a petrol station. I've no doubt he learned a lesson from the attack on Alice – but almost certainly not the lesson the authorities tried – and failed – to teach him.

On August 3rd 2011, the police were called to Jamie's work. He'd taken a shine to a colleague, but when she told him for the umpteenth time she wasn't interested, he stormed off in a huff, got into his car and reversed it at speed into hers. When he got out of his own car, Jamie was upset and threatening to kill himself. His workmates took pity on him and saw him safely home. The police turned up at the house hours later, and even though they'd been told about Jamie being spurned by his colleague, in less than an hour they'd batted the incident away as a road traffic accident. No further investigation. No checks on Jamie's previous offending.

"It is clear that had this matter been looked into in more detail it would have highlighted Reynold's ongoing and developing behaviour and the need for serious concern about the risks he posed," Julie wrote.

So many chances to stop Jamie in his tracks – all wasted.

Until reading this report, I don't think I'd quite been able to believe all the hints of West Mercia's failures drip-fed to us by our various police sources, or inferred from their telling silences when we asked difficult questions. But now we had it in black and white.

And Julie's probe had gone even further: now we knew how all these other agencies had failed us as well. Reading her findings left me feeling physically battered and bruised. So many people had recognised the danger Jamie posed – but still he was left free and largely unsupervised to attack again. I couldn't get my head around it. Georgia's death and our life sentence of suffering could have so easily been avoided.

"Can't we sue them? I want to sue them all!" I seethed. Not for the money – but to make them hurt. I even sought Frank's advice. He told me we didn't have a chance in hell.

"Not unless you're OK with selling your house – because that's what it'll come to," he said.

"There must be a way," I said.

"It'll ruin you, and all you'll get at the end is, 'we've learned lessons. We won't do it again.'"

Later, Steve and I were invited to Telford and Wrekin Council offices to meet representatives of all the agencies that had been involved with Jamie. It was a long room, with the sun blazing in through the windows, the heat adding to the oppressive atmosphere. There must have been about twenty people there, but on this occasion – unlike at Crown Court – I wasn't intimidated. I felt empowered by Julie Masters' inquiry. We'd been asking for it for ages, and it simply validated what we'd been saying had gone wrong.

As I sat down, I took a deep breath and reminded myself: *you're in the right, they're all here to explain how their departments messed up.* I could see how uncomfortable they were, that they really didn't know how to begin explaining how they'd failed. A lot of them were genuinely upset and remorseful. Not the guy from the YOS, though. I took an instant dislike to him. He was a pompous little man who could barely bring himself to look at us, let alone take responsibility for his staff's actions – or lack of them.

I remember Steve had a question for him. "Who checks the files when a decision is made to prosecute, or caution or issue a warning?" he said.

"The officer passes it on to a civilian worker in that department," the YOS guy replied.

"And what do these civilian workers know about the law?" Steve asked.

"Nothing. They rely on the officer's recommendations."

Steve shook his head at him as I butted in. "What qualifications do the officers need? How are they selected to work in youth offending?"

"We take whoever they send us," he shrugged.

In other words, they're just a bunch of kids who want an easy life, I thought. *They haven't got a clue how to handle someone like Jamie Reynolds.*

The people from the other departments were apologetic. One woman working for Children's Services burst into tears as she explained how they always expected the police to call for a MAPPA – even though any of the departments could do it. Because that didn't happen, it didn't hit home just how serious Jamie's case was. As she choked back her sobs, her manager stepped in, explaining that all the relevant departments were undergoing training so they'd feel confident to call in a MAPPA in the future.

The overall message was just as Frank Mullane had suggested: *We've learned from our mistakes.* Families in our position must get sick of hearing this cliche, because there's rarely any real action to back it up. But later, after the meeting, a woman from Children's Services took me aside and said, "Lynnette – I wanted to show you something…"

She had a poster, with Georgia's photo at the top, and some text below warning kids to trust their instincts and alert an adult if anyone made them feel uncomfortable. They were planning to display them in schools and colleges, and staff would be receiving training to recognise potential victims – as well as perpetrators like Jamie hidden in their midst.

"I wanted to get your feedback on it," she said. "Do you think it's appropriate?"

I had to admit – it was powerful. "I think it's really good," I told her.

"I'd like to get you involved in our training sessions – and the Safeguarding Board, too – if you're agreeable."

"Thank you, I'd like that," I said.

She wanted me to see they were being proactive, that they were taking their responsibilities seriously – and to give them credit, they really were. It was just unbearably sad and painful – and it makes me angry to this day – that Georgia's murder had to be the 'mistake' they learned their lesson from.

I left that meeting feeling heartened that real change was in progress. There was work to do. I could really help ensure the mistakes that cost Georgia her life never happened again. After months of torment, it was a fleetingly brief bit of positivity.

Brief because regardless of any progress we were making, Jamie Reynolds still had a trick or two up his sleeve. He'd been pulling strings for years, and a whole life sentence wasn't about to stop him. I'd thought he was out of the picture, tucked away in HMP Wakefield, for the rest of his days. But he'd been there barely four months – and already he was making a bid for freedom.

FIFTEEN

"You're not going to like this," Hoppy began.

My heart sank. This phrase had prefaced so much bad news, rabbit punches softening me up for the big blow. I braced myself. It landed heavily – none of us had seen it coming. Hoppy had his ear to the ground through work and he'd picked up some information via the Probation Service fresh out of Wakefield prison. The words knocked the wind right out of me. Blood rushed in my ears, a fever-pitch howl...

Jamie Reynolds was appealing against his whole life sentence.

"He's doing what?!" I said.

"I know," Hoppy said. "We can't believe it either."

"There must be something we can do!"

But there wasn't. A couple of weeks later, probation got in touch and put some more flesh on the bones of Hoppy's revelation. Jamie was basing his appeal on his young age, and the fact he'd pleaded guilty. As if he'd had any other choice!

"Do we get a say?" I asked probation. Surely the voices of victims and their families would count for something? I was wrong – we had no rights whatsoever. Beyond making an impact statement, we weren't allowed any input. For now, it was a waiting game. All we could do was hope the judges saw sense.

A follow-up letter from the CPS contained another dose of bitter irony. It explained how Jamie had been planning to appeal using – get this – human rights laws. I could have punched a hole through the kitchen table.

"Blimmin' human rights again!" I screamed. "What about Georgia's human rights!"

The previous summer, the European Court of Human Rights in Strasbourg had ruled whole life tariffs like Jamie's were unlawful, on the basis that they broke laws banning torture. The court said that because there was no chance of release, a whole life sentence amounted to 'inhuman or degrading treatment or punishment'. To my mind, three square meals a day and a cushy jail cell was nothing like as inhuman or degrading as being murdered, raped and dumped naked in the woods – but of course what I thought mattered little in the grand scheme of things. Like me, the UK government also disagreed with Strasbourg. Around the time Steve had gone back to work, Appeal Court judges in London ruled whole life sentences *were* compatible with human rights laws, because there was always a minuscule chance that, in extreme circumstances, they could be reduced by the government.

If Jamie had been looking to Strasbourg to weasel his way out of his punishment, that door had been slammed shut in his face. But now it seemed he'd found another way, and it felt like we'd been slapped back down to square one. We'd waited half a year to see Jamie locked away, supposedly forever. He'd served a little over four months and now he was calling the shots again, trying to control us, snatch another little bit of limelight. Questions looped around and around in my head as I lay in bed at night, and they were still there the next morning, unanswered, to jolt me awake.

How long would this drag on for? How many months – years even – do we have to have this hanging over our heads? What are his chances? And what if the appeal judge shows leniency?

I was overcome with the same dread I'd carried in the run-up to the court case: the possibility that perhaps, in my lifetime, or in Scarlett's, Jamie could be walking the streets again. I imagined turning a corner and finding myself face-to-face with him. I thought of him getting married, raising kids – all those milestones he'd deprived Georgia of. It lurked constantly in the back of my mind. We were in limbo once more.

This bombshell news couldn't have come at a more painfully emotional time, almost as though it had been timed to exact maximum suffering on us. Just a few weeks later marked a year since we'd lost Georgia.

I'd been dreading May 26th. Still do, and always will. If Georgia had died because of – say – an illness or an accident, we might one day have reached some level of acceptance. But she'd been snatched away from us, and suffered such a horrendous death, her loss was impossible to even comprehend, let alone accept.

As the day approached, our sadness gathered weight. Getting up each morning and falling asleep at night were even more of an ordeal than usual. On the day itself, we shuffled between the sofa and the kettle in floods of tears, absolutely lost again, before gathering the strength to drive around to Avondale Road to leave some flowers. After tying a bouquet to the lamppost, I turned to look at the house, haunted again by visions of what had happened inside it. Jamie's family had moved out after Georgia's murder, and now it stood still and empty.

I'd felt sorry for Jamie's parents at first, before we realised they'd known for years that he was looking at torture pornography. Within a week of Georgia's murder, I even slipped a sympathy card to the vicar to pass on to Jamie's mum.

I'm so sorry, you're in an awful position too. We don't hold you responsible. I hope you're coping OK, I wrote inside.

It was heartfelt and genuine, from one lost mother to another. I really thought the family would be devastated that Georgia had lost her life at Jamie's hands, murdered and desecrated in their own home.

Inevitably, the house – and the lamppost outside – had become a focal point for our grief. Not just ours. Georgia's friends', too. Flowers, the odd trinket and cuddly toys appeared on the lamppost from time to time. It was hard to imagine anyone wanting to live there ever again after what had happened within its four walls, but as much as I hated it, Steve and I would pop up there to gather flowers from the doorstep, or sweep up the browning leaves that gathered in the corners of the porch. I hated seeing sad, wilted flowers, so I always took them down from the lamppost within a few days, before they turned.

Even so, the flowers had become a bone of contention, and even this simple act of remembrance had begun causing us problems. There'd been times they'd actually been removed from the lamppost as quickly as we put them up. I couldn't believe anyone could be so insensitive. As if we didn't have enough on our minds.

One day, we'd been to check out Lilleshall country house for a charity ball the Trust was organising. We hadn't long arrived home when the phone rang. I answered to my mum, sounding het up.

"We've just been round to Avondale to leave some flowers, and I thought I'd better warn you – we've had a bit of a row with the stepdad," she said.

She meant Jamie's stepdad, Shaun Thomas. "What's happened?" I said.

"Your dad went to put a little posy up on the lamppost and Shaun came out to have words."

Dad hadn't set a foot on Reynolds' property, and he'd tied the flowers high up on the lamppost like we'd advised, so they didn't end up getting kicked around the street.

"How did Dad take that?" I asked. I could well imagine.

"He said he'd been looking for an excuse to punch someone for months and suggested Shaun went back inside," Mum said. "I think Shaun's calling the police."

"All right, we'll handle it," I said.

A while later, there was a knock at the door. It was one of the inspectors from Wellington police station, Gary Wade.

"We've had a complaint about you putting flowers on the lamppost at Avondale Road," he said.

"What sort of time was this?" Steve said. "Because I can guarantee it wasn't us – we've been over at Lilleshall."

Then I stepped in. "Steve's right. It wasn't us – in fact it was my mum and dad." What was he going to do? Arrest a couple of pensioners for leaving flowers for their dead granddaughter? "It's the first time they've been," I said. "We've told people to calm it down with the flowers because we know Jamie's family don't like it."

"This really isn't a police matter," Steve told Wade. "But you can tell them this – there's only going to be flowers there on Georgia's birthday, the day she was murdered, and Christmas. That's it."

"Our daughter's been murdered and raped around the house, and they're bothered by some flowers on a lamppost?" I spat. "What are they on about?"

This went round and round between us, Jamie's family and the police for months. Inspector Wade took it upon himself to try and act as some kind of mediator.

"So, how are we going to resolve this?" he said on one occasion.

"We're not resolving anything!" I told him. "That's what we're doing, and that's the end of it. We're not on their property, we're not doing it to rub their noses in it – it's simply for us, to remember Georgia."

"Wouldn't you be better off leaving flowers on the bench?" Wade suggested.

"She wasn't killed there!" Steve said. "And in any case – the bench was put in Bowring by her friends."

Wade just didn't seem to comprehend the significance.

"Look – it's not a religious thing, but it is a spiritual thing," Steve said. "We put flowers on the lamppost because that house was the last place Georgia lived on this earth. If somehow she can still see us, she'll know those flowers are for her, that we're thinking of her."

I didn't get what was so difficult for everyone to understand, but it meant that even though he was locked up, the spectre of Jamie Reynolds was still tormenting us, still grinding us down. He was 120 miles away, inside a Category A Prison – but somehow he still had a hold over our lives.

Hoppy had paid him another visit to have one last stab at locating Georgia's missing phone and jewellery, and reported back to us looking crestfallen. He'd basically pleaded with Jamie – which made me cross in a way because I didn't want him to think he was getting to us – but his efforts had been futile.

"He's still insisting he chucked them in a bin," Hoppy said.

"I don't believe him for a second. He's kept them for trophies," I said. "He knows where they are."

"I tried to get through to him," Hoppy explained. "I asked him straight – 'is there anything you'd like to say to Steve and Lynnette?' He just shook his head and said 'no'. 'Are you sure?' I said. Still no. 'Come on,' I said. 'Just tell us where this stuff is.' He just wasn't having it. 'Already told you,' he said. 'It went in the bin.'"

He'd tried, but he wasn't getting anywhere. Hoppy had got up to leave and, as he was walking out the door, he'd turned to Jamie and said: "One last time, is there anything you want to say to Steve and Lynnette?"

Jamie replied: "Well, I suppose I ought to say I'm so sorry."

"Sorry?" Hoppy asked him.

"Yeah. Because she was a friend."

As though it wouldn't have mattered if she'd been a stranger he'd picked up on the street. Somehow he even managed to make that about himself – she was *his* friend.

After leaving the bouquet at Avondale, we slipped back home and sat sobbing once more. In the end I suggested: "Let's take some flowers up to Georgia's bench as well."

I thought it might help to have a quiet few moments with our thoughts in the open air at Bowring. It had to be better than sitting in the house crying.

"Yeah, come on," Steve agreed.

Scarlett and Maxine joined us, and we set off for the park together, each lost in our thoughts and memories of Georgia. Then, nearing the bench, we realised it was thronged with people – Georgia's friends and their families. Some had driven from the other side of Telford and as far away as Wolverhampton. Flowers, little candles and even cans of beer adorned the bench. Lads from the local bands sat around on the grass, singing and strumming guitars. People from all walks of life – from long-haired rockers to smartly dressed posh kids – shared memories of Georgia, or released balloons and Chinese lanterns in her memory. News of Jamie's appeal wasn't lost on them, and among the kind words and condolences there was some choice language flying around. No one could believe he had the audacity to heap even more hurt on us all. Seeing all that happening and knowing Georgia was still in hearts and minds took the edge off what was always going to be a desperately sad day. We'd only planned to nip over but by the time we headed home, dusk was falling and the lanterns were points of flickering orange light fading into the distance.

It got to June 2014. Just over a year had passed since Georgia's murder and an announcement from West Mercia Police sparked an emotion which we'd had little cause to experience in the preceding 12 months. There'd been tears, anger, frustration and heart-wrenching grief. Now we felt a glimmer of hope. The force was going to be investigated by officers from Devon and Cornwall Police. Finally, some accountability was on the horizon. West Mercia's failings would be laid bare in black and white so the public could judge for themselves. Even though Jamie's earlier brushes with the law had been revealed in court, I still felt it hadn't punched through that Georgia's murder was far from an isolated incident, that instead it had been the realisation of a demented fantasy the police knew Jamie had harboured for years. Devon and Cornwall would set the record straight.

Karen Manners was already thinking about the future, about how West Mercia's officers could learn from Georgia's story.

"When all this is done and dusted, I want to get you involved in live training sessions, especially with the new recruits," she told us. "I think it could be really impactful."

She had no idea what was coming, or that Devon and Cornwall's inquiry would prove so damning. When she'd tearfully thrown down that file in the MAPPA report meeting months earlier, telling us how ashamed she felt, I'm not sure even she realised just how poor West Mercia's 2008 investigation into Jamie Reynolds had been.

I'd been dreading the appointment of a neighbouring police force to carry out the probe. I didn't want any lingering questions over impartiality. The news that it was Devon and Cornwall came as a massive relief. The two officers heading up the inquiry – codenamed Operation Columbia – visited us at home to introduce themselves. DCI David Prywata was a big bear of a man with a self assurance to match his size. I couldn't imagine much getting past him. He came across as absolutely determined. With him was Sergeant Gerry Mudge, another sizeable bloke, tall with glasses. He had a calming manner which instantly put me at ease.

"We will dig deep," Prywata said. "They might not like us up here, but we'll get the information we want."

"We've got a solid team of detectives doing the enquiries," Mudge added. They were running it like a criminal investigation – taking statements, combing through records, following email trails and picking over police pocket book entries.

"We did the briefing, told the team everything that had gone wrong and explained it's our job to find out why," said Prywata. "I must tell you – there was a lot of bad language flying around the room. They couldn't believe the circumstances."

"No. Nor could we," I said.

"Well – we want to answer all your questions, and I'm sure you'll have a lot of them," Prywata replied. He hadn't even begun yet, but Prywata already seemed visibly shocked by what he knew. "We'll keep you both updated as we go along. I had a word with a few people at Malinsgate and everyone speaks very highly of you, Steve. As much as I can, I want to share with you what we're up to. If you think we've missed something, just let me know. We'll go back, we'll ask again."

Clearly he had the same high standards as Steve. He could see we'd been let down enough, and he wasn't going to let it happen again on his watch.

"Yes, of course," said Steve. "And thank you."

These two Devon and Cornwall cats were now among the pigeons at West Mercia. It had taken almost a year to get to this point. West Mercia had wanted it. We needed it. Prywata and Mudge had promised to leave no stone unturned, and not everyone was going to like what – and who – they found underneath.

SIXTEEN

Dick Langton looked like he wanted to disappear down the back of our sofa. He seemed to be folding in on himself, deflating as though he had a slow puncture.

Is he going to cry? I thought, catching a tremble in his bottom lip and a moist sheen to his eyes. *Please don't start crying!*

Since his promotion to Chief Inspector, Dick had been making noises about stepping down from his role as chair of the Georgia Williams Trust. The charity had been his idea and to be fair to Dick, it had proved a good one. In less than a year, it had raised over £50k. We'd given out scores of grants to local youngsters, sent kids from New College on a charity mission to remote villages in Morocco, and we were already making plans for a second Ferret Fest music festival. On a personal level, for Steve, Scarlett and I, it had been a lifeline. As well as giving us focus, it kept us in touch with Georgia's friends. Often it provided a fun reason to leave the house when we could have easily stayed at home, weighed down by our grief.

But for Dick, it seemed the pressures and responsibilities of his new position in West Mercia Police had made him rethink his role as Trust chair. As his workload increased he'd been suggesting I take over. Now, he'd brought his wife along to ours to plead his case for him. She sat forward, perched on the edge of the sofa, as Dick seemed to shrivel pathetically behind her.

"He can't do it all," she implored. "It's too much for him. He needs help."

"We've been telling him he's doing too much," I said. "The other trustees are more than willing to help out. He needs to delegate, get the others involved – we don't want them to lose their enthusiasm."

I explained I felt ready to take on more responsibility, but it felt to me like Dick was avoiding eye contact for some reason, as though there was more behind this than just his full plate at work. Whatever was preying on his mind, he wasn't letting on.

Now that the Devon and Cornwall investigation was underway in West Mercia, Steve found the atmosphere at work increasingly hostile. All the officers who'd been involved with Jamie Reynolds back in 2008 would have had an idea of what was coming – but now it was actually happening, and noses were being knocked out of joint left, right and centre. At first, although he had a few suspicions, Steve couldn't be sure which officers were about to find themselves blinking in the glare of Devon and Cornwall's spotlight. At times, it made the working day unbearably awkward. He never knew when he might run into one of them, or find himself standing next to one as they queued for lunch in the staff canteen. One evening he was leaving work for the day, walking down the stairwell with Steve Tonks. As the pair of them reached the next landing, they were joined by a uniformed police woman. Steve struck up a brief conversation with her – the usual end-of-the-day small talk – and as they reached the ground floor they all went their separate ways.

A couple of weeks later, Steve and Tonks were chatting when the Devon and Cornwall probe came up.

"You really haven't got a clue who these people are, have you?" Tonks said to him.

Steve shook his head. "I've got an inkling about a couple of them based on how they've been with me – but no, nothing concrete."

"I didn't think so," Tonks said. "You know what convinced me? The other day when we were walking downstairs with the girl in uniform…"

"Yeah…"

"She's one of them."

Steve was gobsmacked. It turned out the officer was called Faye Osmund-Smith. She was the police constable who'd gone and interviewed Alice after she was attacked, and who went on to arrest and interview Jamie.

On another occasion, Steve got invited to start playing football again with some of the lads after work. They split up into two teams and had a kick around, but Steve noticed a guy on the opposing team was unusually quiet.

He mentioned a name to me. "I know him from uniform days. He's with Youth Offending. He barely said a word all match, and when we all went to shake hands after, he grabbed his kit up from behind the goal and scurried off."

"You think he's one of them Devon and Cornwall want to question?"

"It's got me wondering," Steve said.

The same guy played the following week, but again came across as oddly withdrawn. Steve said after that he never showed up again.

There were other sad, petty, little moments which heaped added pressure onto Steve – pressure he could have done without. Like the remembrance poem he wrote for Georgia and pinned to one of the noticeboards in the stairwell at Malinsgate. Steve poured his emotion onto the page. His verse was simply a tribute to Georgia and an attempt to put an unfathomable loss into words. Yet within hours of the poem going up, it was taken down – and Steve was summoned for a chat with the boss. It had hit a nerve at work and, from then on, Steve resolved to post a fresh copy of his poem to the noticeboard on Georgia's birthday, at Christmas, and on the anniversary of her murder. Each time, the poem would vanish. I couldn't believe anyone would be so petty as to take offence at that, to try to make it about themselves. Sometimes we'd try to laugh off the pettiness because it was so ridiculous, but deep down I could see it really hurt Steve, because work had been like family to him – and now he felt like he was being stabbed in the back. It was grinding him down. He didn't need it. Neither of us did. And it wasn't about to get any better.

"We'll be serving papers on these officers in the next few weeks," Prywata told us. 'Serving papers' is the first stage in the police disciplinary process. It means officers are called in for an interview to explain their version of events. I didn't want to push it, so I didn't ask who. And in any case, we were going to find out soon enough.

Five days after Georgia should have turned 19, we held the second Ferret Fest at Bowring Park, as a celebration of her short life. This year, the Georgia Williams Trust stand was returning bigger and better, and a few of us had agreed to man it, working in a rota.

"I'll go over early and lend a hand setting up," I told Steve.

"OK, I'll be over in a bit," he said.

I walked on to the car park at Bowring where kids were unloading armfuls of pre-blown balloons from the backs of cars. Spotting Dick Langton in his white Trust T-shirt with the orange ferret emblazoned on the front, I wandered over to say hello.

"Morning!" I said, cheery as anything.

But Dick's face soured and he blanked me.

An awkward moment passed. I didn't know where to put myself. "Is there anything I can do to help?" I said.

Dick shrugged me off. "I'm going to set the stall up."

Blimmin' heck, I thought. *Someone got out of bed on the wrong side this morning.*

I didn't push it, and instead followed grumpy Dick over to our spot by the park gates. As we wrestled with a gazebo, Dick was far from his usual, chatty, Mr Nice Guy self. Instead he was frosty and withdrawn, his eyes darting nervously to avoid mine. When he did manage a smile, it seemed tight and forced – not at all the smug grin I was used to. By the time the gazebo was up, I'd had enough of the cold-shoulder treatment and went to chat with a few other stallholders.

A while later, Steve turned up. Dick still had a face on, and when he was out of earshot, I said to Steve out of the corner of my mouth: "Dick's in a right mood about something."

"I noticed that too," Steve said. "What's up with him?"

I shrugged. "Your guess is as good as mine."

"Well – I'll leave you to it. I'm going to have a wander round the stalls to thank everyone for coming."

While Steve was gone, he bumped into a retired officer. She'd got wind of the impending disciplinary and wanted to know how it was going.

"Where are they up to?" she asked Steve.

"They're getting ready to serve papers," he told her.

Some of the names of the likely officers were already common knowledge if you were in the right circles – which this ex-cop clearly was. And she had plenty to say about one of them.

Steve set off walking back to our stand. As he crossed the grass I could tell by his demeanour something had wound him up. Dick stood next to me watching him as he stalked towards us, face like thunder and muttering under his breath. By the time he'd reached us he looked fit to explode.

"Fucking them lot," he hissed, huffing and puffing. "Bunch of lazy bastards!"

He stomped and seethed for a bit, before Langton suddenly snapped. "You want to back off, Steve. Leave it alone and back off!"

Steve froze. "What are you on about?" he said.

"You're not going to get what you want!"

Steve took a step back, astonished. "How the fuck do you know what I want?" he said. "And what the fuck's it got to do with you anyway?"

Langton took a breath, wrestling with himself. "OK. I suppose I'd better tell you now. I was the squad's inspector the night Jamie Reynolds tried to strangle that girl."

"You what?"

"Yeah. I'm expecting papers in the next week or two."

Steve was stunned into silence. Neither of us could believe what we were hearing. It was such an astonishing betrayal, another knife between the shoulder blades from someone who was meant to be supporting us.

Then Dick turned to me. "You need to calm him down. He's not going to get what he wants," he said.

"You don't know what he wants," I told him.

"He wants us sacked! He wants all the officers sacked! But being angry isn't going to get him anywhere."

"Sorry, but I'm with Steve on this one – I want you all sacked as well."

With that, Dick turned tail and scurried away.

He hadn't been 'on the periphery' at all. He'd been right there at the heart of it. This revelation cast a shadow over everything he'd done in the last year. I'd been only too happy for Dick – a trusted officer, rising in the ranks – to put his name to the charity. But now I had to wonder – was it damage limitation so he wouldn't look as bad if everything blew up in his face? Was he trying to make amends, or to ease a guilty conscience?

Dick had wanted to step back from the Georgia Williams Trust for a while, and in my mind this latest news made his position untenable. At the close of the trustees' next monthly meeting, Dick launched into a resignation speech, citing his new police role and the extra workload. Meanwhile I bit my tongue, keeping what I knew to myself but privately thinking, *you smarmy little…* It was an awful feeling. *Just go,* I thought. *I don't want you here anymore. You could have come to us months ago and laid all your cards on the table.* Instead, he'd let it get this far, embarrassing us all. His name, his photo in the local papers, would be linked to the charity forever. I felt like he'd sullied it – and Georgia's memory – by letting her down. For the time being, I rose above it. I didn't want to come across as vindictive. I wanted Dick to know I was better than him, so I smiled through his leaving coffees and cake at the end of the meeting, and thanked him for all he'd done, even handing him a framed print as a parting gift from us all.

"He took it then?" Steve said later.

"Yes, he took it."

Steve shook his head. "Unbelievable. No scruples whatsoever."

In the meantime, six officers had been served misconduct papers – Delahay and Osmund-Smith among them. Dick Langton's name joined the list a few weeks later. We'd placed all our faith in Prywata, Mudge and the police disciplinary process. All I could do was hope that Dick Langton's time would come. But now there was another day of reckoning on the horizon. Jamie Reynolds' case was being heard in the Court of Appeal.

SEVENTEEN

The cavernous entrance to the Royal Courts of Justice yawned in front of us. As Steve and I climbed the steps, a wave of nausea hit me. This building looked more like a palace than a courthouse, with towering steeples and tall windows, as though it had been built to intimidate. If so, it had achieved its purpose. I felt tiny. Even more so walking through the archway into the Great Hall. Our footsteps echoed on the ornate mosaic tiles. Huge, vaulted ceilings soared above us. Antique oil paintings hung on the walls. The whole place was so steeped in history, you could smell it in the air. Normally I could have spent an age just gazing at the artwork and architecture. But not today – I was too nervous. It was October 16th 2014 and we were there to listen to three Court of Appeal judges hear arguments why – and why not – Jamie deserved to have his whole life sentence reduced.

We'd been on tenterhooks for the previous few weeks, petrified that the judges might show Jamie leniency. It was impossible to imagine anyone taking sides with a dangerous, sadistic killer like him, but nonetheless we felt like we were back at square one, almost as though we were waiting for the trial again – only this time we had a good idea what was coming. The tension, the constant churn in my guts, was unbearable.

Compared with Stafford Crown, the Court of Appeal was altogether grander and more formal. The setting magnified the seriousness of the occasion. As we waited in one of the family rooms, I knew the barristers would be sharpening their tongues for another battle of wits and legal knowledge. At stake was Jamie's future, and our peace of mind.

A few weeks before, the barrister for the Crown – the guy on 'our' side – had invited us to London to talk through the appeal process. His confidence and determination to make sure the whole life sentence stuck had been reassuring.

"Is there anything you'd like to say?" he asked.

"I've got a few things," Steve said.

The barrister explained that, in court, all we could do was watch. Nonetheless, we could write another impact statement to put before that judge. A week before the hearing, Steve did just that – and he didn't pull any punches.

Where is Georgia's right to appeal? he wrote. *Where is our right to appeal against this life sentence that I can only describe as purgatory?*

Then, he addressed Jamie directly: *Rot in hell you inhuman excuse for a life. I hope every day for you is full of the grief that twists my stomach into knots, that fills me with fear and apprehension, that makes me physically sick, that has no hope of ever going away, but eats further and further into you as each second of the day goes by.*

I hope you cry yourself to sleep every night and wake every morning with the same stinging tears that burn into my eyes. I just wish that you could experience the torture that I go through every day without hope of even a moment's relief. Your heart should be ripped to shreds like mine, your waking moments restless without peace or solace, your life empty – only then you may get somewhere near to what I feel, and what torments me with never-ending frustration.

Once more, Steve had captured our emotions with devastating, heartbreaking accuracy.

I still felt sick as we took a seat in one of the courtroom pews, along with Tonks and Hoppy who were there to represent the police. Never in a million years would I have thought that one day I'd find myself sat in the High Court. The solemn and oppressive atmosphere bore down on us. How much anguish and sadness had these four walls witnessed, I wondered? They would have seen their fair share of winners and losers. We could only hope the scales of justice tipped in our favour today.

We already knew Jamie wouldn't be attending in person, and I swivelled to glance at the video link screen the usher had pointed out to us. For the time being, it was still blank. But Jamie would be appearing on it in a live feed from HMP Wakefield. As the hearing got underway, the screen blinked into life – and there was Jamie. He looked a little heavier, his hair was cut short and the goatee beard was gone. I willed him to look into the camera – the closest I'd get to eye-to-eye contact – but I knew in reality that while we could see him, he couldn't see us. Jamie could listen, and respond, but the video link was one-way only. *He should be made to face us,* I thought. *We're only here because of him.* I scoured his face for any sign of remorse. As before, I saw none. Jamie's features remained impassive, his head slightly bowed and his eyes cast to the ground. The only time he spoke was to confirm his name.

His barrister set out a two-pronged argument. Firstly, he said Jamie wasn't given enough credit for pleading guilty. *Eventually pleading guilty,* I thought. He could have done it in June and spared us six months of torment while we had a trial hanging over our heads. Apparently saving us from hearing all the evidence, even at that late stage, had been a 'mercy'. What a joke. It was a mercy so small it was microscopic.

The other excuse was the same old chestnut he'd used in court – that Georgia was *only just* a child in the eyes of the law. It was like groundhog day. The argument made zero sense. You can't start driving at sixteen and three quarters because you're *almost* 17. You don't get to buy alcohol because you're turning 18 in a month's time. The law is the law. It was all we could do to stop ourselves from leaping to our feet and screaming: *She was a child! She was* our *child!* It wouldn't have mattered if she'd been 17 years and 364 days old – she'd still have been a child.

The judges called an adjournment, with an instruction for Hoppy: they wanted to see the photos of Georgia's murder. High Court was as new for Hoppy as it was for us. He looked a little flustered but while the court adjourned he dashed off to get the files together, then slipped into the judges' chambers to talk them through the photos.

"What do you think?" Steve asked when he returned.

"We went through everything in detail," Hoppy said. "They looked appalled."

Who wouldn't be? Only someone with a heart of stone could look at those images and fail to be moved, disgusted and horrified. Surely they were reason enough to keep Jamie locked up forever?

It was an agonising two-week wait for the ruling. Even the hardened officers of West Mercia's Major Investigation Unit were nervous. As usual, we heard first through the work grapevine: Jamie would indeed die behind bars. I shook with relief at the news.

"It's over?"

"It's over," Steve said.

It was a huge weight off our shoulders, one less battle to fight. Later, in a nine-page document, the judges explained their decision. I didn't read it at the time because it went into some detail about Georgia's death, and I've survived by not knowing all the facts. I never want to know all the facts. But the most important bits – the bits that meant Jamie would be staying in prison forever – came at the end.

Reynolds did not admit he committed the killing until a few days before the trial. The evidence was overwhelming and we can find nothing in the psychiatric evidence that in any way justifies the failure to admit the killing… he showed no remorse.

The fact that Georgia was 17 years old was not a material consideration. Parliament provided that she was to be considered as a child… There is no basis on which it can be properly argued that a whole life order was not required. The application is refused.

As long as Jamie had a whole life sentence, I felt like I could cope. I didn't have to waste any more thought or energy on him. He was out of the way, for good.

By now, we'd been sitting on the MAPPA report for months and we still desperately wanted its findings made public. Meeting with Assistant Chief Constable Karen Manners to discuss next steps, she made West Mercia's stance on the matter abundantly clear – they were fully intent on keeping their dirty secret to themselves.

"We want to learn from this," Karen said. "We want to use it to guide our training, and we'd like you to be involved."

"That sounds good," Steve said. "Of course we want to be involved however we can."

Perhaps Karen thought that would be enough to appease us. By now, she really should have known better.

"When do you think you'll be ready to publish the report?" Steve said, without batting an eyelid.

Karen looked taken aback. "We think it'd be better if it was kept in-house."

Yeah, I bet you do, I thought. "Well – no," I said. "We want it published."

"I've spoken to the chief and no one's mentioned publishing it. If you were to work with us…"

I stopped her there. "You can either publish it officially, or I'll do it myself," I said.

"You can't do that."

"I can. I've got my copy and I can give it to whoever I want. I'll give it to the press if I have to."

Steve nodded. "We'll do everything we can to make sure it sees the light of day."

Karen's face darkened, like the sun had been smothered by storm clouds.

"But going back to this training," Steve said. "Who's going to speak to the recruits from a police officer's point of view? You need someone who can tell it as it is, someone with experience."

Karen looked at Steve for a long moment, and then said: "Well, we don't want any silver-haired, crusty old detectives, do we, Steve?"

"You wouldn't be referring to me, would you?" Steve asked her.

Karen just smiled and looked down.

"Regardless, I'm with Lynnette," Steve told her. "We'll see that report published."

At that, Karen got to her feet. "You can go ahead and have your day in the press," she said. "But just remember – today's news is tomorrow's fish and chip paper."

It had been months of struggle to get to where we were, but still the fight was far from done, and at this point Steve and I were both exhausted, running on empty. Steve's job as a police officer had been a blessing in one way – without his inside knowledge, we wouldn't have stood a chance. But at the same time, the pressure of juggling work and battling for the truth, coupled with the atmosphere at Malinsgate – the complaints and back-biting – were all taking their toll.

I was at home one day when a car pulled up outside and Steve and Hoppy got out. Hoppy led Steve into the house, looked at me and shook his head.

"What's happened?" I queried. "Steve?"

He was ashen-faced, his shoulders slumped. He looked physically ill.

"He's not good," Hoppy said. "How he's being treated at work – it's not fair. I'm responsible for his welfare, and on this occasion I thought it only right I bring him home."

Later, Steve filled me in on what had happened. A week earlier, we'd had to report yet another case of flowers going missing from Avondale Road.

"Gary Wade called me today and said he wanted a word about it," Steve said. "So he comes up to MIU and we go into one of the offices."

Wade had told Steve that the Reynolds family might make a complaint.

"I told him fine," Steve said. "We're not going to stop leaving flowers. I said I'd stand my ground in court if it came to it."

"Fair enough," I said.

"Yeah – but then he started going on about the officers Devon and Cornwall are looking at, asking where they're getting all the evidence from. And I'm thinking – what's it got to do with him? What's he quizzing me about this for?"

Steve had blown his top at him. *What's your fucking agenda? You supposedly called me in here to talk about flowers and now you're grilling me about Devon and Cornwall's investigation. What are you playing at?*

"He goes, 'I haven't got an agenda,' so I told him, 'You fucking well have – and another thing, those officers under investigation are just incompetent. They could have seized Reynolds' computer off him and re-arrested him.' So then he says, 'Well that wouldn't have been proportionate or legal.'"

That was the last straw for Steve, he'd told Wade to F-off and stormed out – unaware that Hoppy had overheard the argument. Worried for Steve's mental health – seeing him wound up to breaking point – Hoppy had gently stepped in and brought him home.

"What happens now?" I said.

In recent months, on top of everything else, I'd started worrying whether Steve could survive his return to work. He'd never shied away from speaking his mind, but his fuse was burning shorter and shorter. I was terrified he was either going to lose his rag and get the sack, or grow so weary of the stress and back-biting that he was forced to quit for the sake of his sanity. One way or another, I was convinced they were trying to push him out. But as Steve recovered from this latest showdown, an appointment with the GP granted us a reprieve – he was signed off work for six months on medical grounds.

Steve was a month into this convalescence when Prywata and Mudge called round the house with Hoppy, Tonks and McGee to hand us the results of Operation Columbia – an almost year-long investigation.

"It's all there," said Prywata. "You'll see when you read it properly that we've included some of the comments from the officers' interviews. Frankly, they speak volumes about their attitude."

Steve was thumbing through the report when a sentence caught his eye, something Prywata's team had picked up while interviewing Jo Delahay: *She did not consider that looking for evidence of similar or like offences was proportionate or legal in the circumstances.*

"Hang on," Steve said. "Who else has had this report? Has someone leaked it? Because I've heard this phrase before. 'Proportionate or legal'. Where have I heard that?"

Prywata was absolutely resolute. "I can assure you – no one on my team has leaked anything."

Steve shook his head, trying to dredge up a memory. "I trust you Dave, but I'm telling you – I've heard this before somewhere."

Steve thought for a moment before the penny dropped. "It was Gary Wade! Hoppy, remember that row we had? He said it. He used those exact words – proportionate or legal. What's going on?"

Prywata exchanged a knowing look with Hoppy before ducking out of the room to make a phone call. It was a good half an hour before he returned. "I've been talking to the bosses at your HQ, they've ordered me not to tell you this but I'm not having you think any of my staff have been leaking, and I don't work for West Mercia. Wade is Jo Delahay's Police Federation friend."

Federation 'friends' are like advisors to officers facing disciplinaries. They might help out with statements and can even sit in on interviews.

"You what?" Steve said, flabbergasted. "How can we possibly trust him to do a proper job of investigating these missing flowers when he's batting for Jo Delahay? I can't believe it." Then he turned to Hoppy. "You knew…"

Hoppy sighed. "I was told not to tell you. Soon as I found out, I could see it was going to be a problem. I raised it in work and I was told to keep schtum. I'm sorry, Steve."

To us, it felt like another kick in the teeth. At a time when we needed nothing less than 100% transparency – when our trust in West Mercia Police had hit rock bottom – the waters had been muddied once more.

Later that evening Steve and I sat down to read Operation Columbia's findings together. Just as they'd promised, Prywata and Mudge really had left no stone unturned. Their report ran to eighty-six pages. Although by now we knew or at least suspected many of the key findings, seeing them written in black and white was devastating. In many ways, it was even worse than we'd thought. Nobody had said, "I'm sorry." We'd had to dig in our heels and fight tooth and nail for this inquiry, just to prove what we'd been saying for months – it totally vindicated us.

The upshot was, although the investigation into the terrifying attack on Alice had been 'adequate' for a basic assault, it should have gone further. Much further. The doctored photos, violent pornography and a last-minute confession from Jamie that he was turned on by pictures of women being strangled should have taken the inquiry in an entirely different direction. Although there was some recognition of the risk he posed, little was done to address that risk. Failure after failure meant the decision to give him a final warning was flawed. And three years later, when he rammed his colleague's car, basic police record checks weren't carried out. No one linked this so-called 'traffic accident' to his previous offending.

When Alice's uncle called 999 to report the attack, Police Constable Faye Osmund-Smith was on a late shift at Wellington police station. The incident was given a 'Grade 2 Priority' status, meaning she should have dropped everything and got to Alice's as quickly as she could. Instead, most likely she finished off her emails and paperwork, arriving at Alice's almost an hour later. Within minutes, she'd disregarded the opportunity to arrange a video interview and had started taking a written statement, treating the attack as an 'Actual Bodily Harm' assault. She didn't arrange for forensics or photos of Alice's injuries, and Alice claimed she'd had to press her to take as evidence the messages Jamie sent her telling her to wear knee-high boots for his imaginary photo shoot – a claim Osmund-Smith denied. Shaken and vulnerable, Alice told Osmund-Smith she was going to stay away from college the next day, clearly fearful of running into Jamie. But the officer insisted she tell staff about the assault. This lack of care set the tone for the rest of the inquiry – although the investigation found a note on the case file suggesting that Alice was told about Jamie's final warning, despite her insistence that she never heard from the police again.

Then, when Jamie's doctored pictures came to light a few days after his arrest, Osmund-Smith left them out of the crime report because Alice wasn't in them. The images did rightly worry her, though, and she tried to raise her concerns with the force's Public Protection Unit – but they were unwilling to pick it up.

With better supervision, Osmund-Smith might have stood a fighting chance of doing a decent job. As it was, she had Detective Sergeant Jo Delahay to look to for guidance, and between the pair of them they missed opportunity after opportunity. Delahay joined Osmund-Smith at Jamie's and helped arrest him – but she too completely failed to recognise the seriousness of the attack. It would have just compounded Osmund-Smith's view that Alice had been assaulted. Delahay apparently didn't think it was 'proportionate' to photograph the scene of the crime, or seize Jamie's clothing. Later, when Osmund-Smith raised Jamie's doctored images with her, she said it wasn't a crime to digitally alter photos, or possess them. Overall, Operation Columbia described both her supervision and her investigation as 'poor'.

And then there was Chief Inspector Dick Langton, former chairman of the Georgia Williams Trust. Had it really slipped his mind when he was wheedling his way into our lives that he'd had dealings with the Jamie Reynolds case back in 2008? I'd never know for sure, but I doubted it. On the day Jamie attacked Alice, Dick had been the on-duty Response Inspector. That meant he was responsible for both Osmund-Smith *and* Delahay. Dick even stated he was 'pleased' with how Osmund-Smith handled the investigation, and thought he'd supervised it appropriately. He'd only got involved about three weeks in when Delahay emailed him to raise Osmund-Smith's concerns over the doctored photos. He also contacted the Public Protection Unit, who promised some support – but it wasn't forthcoming. Dick didn't chase it up, and never tried to tip the case up to CID. *Contrary to the issues identified, CI Langton maintains that the incident and images were investigated appropriately,* the Columbia report found.

"The lazy bastard," Steve remarked. "The lot of them – they're all lazy bastards."

With the cursory investigation into the attack on Alice all sewn up, the file was evaluated by an Evidence Review Manager, in this case a civilian police worker called Louise Hill. She gave it the green light for a warning, subject to a final assessment by the Youth Offending Team – a flawed decision, the report said, based on an incomplete investigation. Hill had also failed to spot the link between the seized violent pornography and Alice being strangled. Despite everything that had followed, Hill told Columbia she still felt a final warning for Jamie had been appropriate.

There was one last checkpoint where Jamie might have been stopped in his tracks, and manning the gates was Steve's old footballing opponent, who worked with the Youth Offending Team and had completed the final assessment on Jamie to check that his case was indeed suitable for just a warning, rather than a prosecution in court. Two months after the attack, Jamie attended Wellington police station with his parents in tow for an interview with this officer. It would be the first time Jamie really opened up about attacking Alice. He talked about his feelings towards her, admitted he was aroused by strangulation pornography, and confessed to masturbating over his doctored images of Jadine and her pal. Columbia found no evidence that these bombshell new admissions were conveyed to Osmund-Smith or Louise Hill, or submitted as intelligence on the force IT network. Reading that, I burst into tears. You didn't have to be an ace detective to understand the relevance of this information. Even to the ordinary bloke in the street, it would have been blindingly obvious.

Then, three years later, came another squandered opportunity. Operation Columbia gave us the clearest picture to date of Jamie's terrifying response to being spurned by his work colleague. Over the course of six months working at the motorway services in Shifnal,

Jamie developed what was described as an 'obsession' with this poor girl. She'd knocked him back time and again, and even told her bosses that he wouldn't leave her alone. They gave Jamie a talking-to but let him keep his job. And *still* he wouldn't take no for an answer.

He was in the car park with her on August 3rd 2011 when he asked her out yet again. When she said no, he got in his car and reversed at speed into hers. She never actually saw the collision, so when it came to reporting it, she couldn't say for sure it was deliberate – but she *did* tell the attending PC and Acting Sergeant about the history of her fractious work relationship with Jamie. She said the sergeant dismissed the job as 'just a domestic' and questioned why they'd been called at all. A second PC was sent round to Jamie's to do a welfare check and found him more worried about losing his no claims bonus than anything else. None of the officers involved checked the Police National Computer for any previous record of offending. How differently things might have turned out if they had – instead of dealing with the smash as a traffic accident, they could have at least investigated Jamie for harassment. *The use of police system checks could have been beneficial,* Columbia decided.

So, we had the report, West Mercia Police had the report – and now we wanted *everyone* to have the report. Prywata and Mudge agreed it should be published, but it wasn't their call, and until any disciplinary action had concluded, it was unlikely to see the light of day. Columbia had recommended the four officers from 2008, plus the civilian police worker, should face misconduct proceedings. A further three officers were earmarked for 'management action' for poor performance. I thought back to almost two years previously when Tonks and McGee had told us heads would roll. There had to be accountability.

It was now up to Devon and Cornwall Police to decide which officers should be put forward for disciplinary action, and their fate would lie in the hands of West Mercia.

EIGHTEEN

While Steve was off sick, we limped on with a growing sense of dread as our futures began to look more and more uncertain. Weeks then months slipped by. We needed a back-to-work plan, but we could never reach human resources, or were fobbed off with excuses. We tried to arrange a fresh round of therapy with a police counsellor Steve had seen months previously – but in another note of bitter irony, she was now treating the officers facing misconduct action in the fall-out from Operation Columbia. It'd be a conflict of interest for Steve to see her, we were told.

Following advice from the Police Federation, Steve even looked at getting a medical discharge – but the top brass turned him down. I remember calling personnel in a rage. "They can't treat him like this," I told them. "Where's the support?" Often I'd be left on hold for what felt like a lifetime until the line clicked dead. Then, eventually, I was put through to head office at Hindlip Hall. A kindly, female voice answered the phone, and I finally thought I might be getting somewhere. I explained what had been going on and thanked her for listening. Suddenly she went very quiet.

"I know you've rung before and that no one's got back to you," she said. "I'm not trying to make excuses, but we've got no one to deal with welfare – they've all been made redundant."

I was astonished. If everyone in welfare had been laid off, who was looking out for the officers?

We were at the end of our tether. As summer 2015 gave way to autumn, Steve reached a monumental decision: he drafted a letter of resignation and handed his notice in. West Mercia replied within a couple of days – his resignation had been accepted. He'd officially leave in September. All the plans we'd made for the twilight years of our lives were slipping away, like sand running through our fingers. But we couldn't go on as we were. Something had to give.

We'll manage, I told myself. *Somehow we'll manage.* I thought if we could just get through this, the rest might eventually fall into place.

In little time, Steve found a new job as a discipline officer at a local school. Privately, I wasn't sure it was the best role for him. His short fuse had been torched to a blackened stub, and I wasn't convinced his heart was really in it. Despite all the hurt, he was still looking over his shoulder to Malinsgate police station.

It got to the last-day-but-one of Steve's notice. In less than 48 hours, after more than two decades of service, he'd be quitting the force. He was already having doubts about the school job but nonetheless he was at an induction day for his new role when he called me during the lunchbreak.

"How's it going?" I asked.

"I'm not sure I'm going to like this," he said. "I can see myself getting really upset seeing these kids grow up. It's not been the best induction."

"Hang in there for now, we'll work something out," I told him.

But it was already obvious this job was just going to make Steve miserable. His resignation had really been a cry for help. Couldn't West Mercia see that?

In desperation, I called Hoppy. "There must be something you can do..." I said.

He got on to Adrian McGee, who in turn pleaded Steve's case with the bosses, telling them they'd rue the day they lost one of their top detectives.

A couple of hours later, McGee called me back.

"Tell Steve – if he wants to stay in the police, I've had a word and they'll accept him withdrawing his notice," he said. "But HR have got to have that withdrawal by 4.30 this afternoon."

Steve was finishing his induction at 3.30pm. I called him five minutes later and he rushed home, jumped on the computer and with just minutes to spare fired off an email withdrawing his resignation.

He was back in. For now.

It felt to me as though we were teetering on a tightrope. Steve was under pressure now to toe the line, but we were still pressing for West Mercia – and all the other agencies – to face public scrutiny for their failures. I think, in the end, we pestered so much that we became an embarrassment to them. We just wouldn't give in. I'm sure they'd have much rather we'd stood side-by-side with them, sucking it up and sugar-coating their blunders, but that was never going to happen.

In October 2015 – a few weeks after Georgia should have turned 20 – West Mercia Police agreed to hold a press conference to coincide with publishing the MAPPA Discretionary Serious Case Review. Perhaps they saw it as something of a compromise – if they gave us that, we might forget about the Devon and Cornwall report. Perhaps they thought that by holding a press conference, they'd at least be able to have their say and limit the damage.

Scarlett told Jadine about our plans and she was adamant she wanted to be involved. The intervening months had done nothing to diminish her own rage – she was determined to stand up and be counted. She'd been granted lifelong anonymity under a court order when Jamie was dealt with at Stafford Crown Court, but she wrote to the judge and he agreed to rescind the ruling.

"It could have been me," she told us. "It could have been any one of us. I need to do this for me – because they let me down – but also I want to be there for you, because they let Georgia down as well."

A week before, we were invited to a little rehearsal at the Ramada Hotel in Telford town centre. The plan was to get us used to fielding questions and see how the room would be set up. That way, we'd know exactly what we were getting into. The Chief Constable, David Shaw, was there too, and Steve took the opportunity to ask him: "What about this Devon and Cornwall report? When are you going to make it public?"

Steve and I had discussed this. The press conference would be our chance not only to say what we really thought of the police, and how they'd let us down, but also to put them on the spot about publishing Columbia's findings.

Perhaps David Shaw had read Steve's mind. "You're still in the police. Just be careful what you say, Steve," he told him. The implication was clear: *Mind how you go, and remember who's paying your wages.*

We'd fought so hard to get here, but when the day came, this little victory felt as empty and hollow as our lives had become since losing Georgia. As I got dressed, the familiar, churning nausea in my stomach was spiked with dread. I was nervous about getting tongue tied and saying the wrong thing. I hated that we'd been put in the position where we had to do it at all. And I was fretting that Steve might push things too far and end up losing his job. It was a surreal position to find yourself in – sat in front of the press having a go at your bosses.

Steve was coming from work, and he ducked out of the office about half an hour before the start of the conference to meet me and Jadine. We found the main function room absolutely mobbed with media. Of course, I'd known there would be press there – that was the point – but the sheer number took me by surprise. The main TV channels had all sent reporters, as well as national and local newspapers, press agencies and radio stations. At the back and on either side of the room were TV cameras, lenses pointing towards the long table where Steve, Jadine and I would face the reporters, alongside David Shaw.

My tummy was still churning as we took our seats in front of the reporters. The table between us and them bristled with microphones. Steve and I sat at one end, then there was Laura Johnston, who headed up children and family services at Telford & Wrekin Council. David Shaw was in the middle, followed by Jadine.

As we expected, there were apologies and promises from Shaw that lessons had been learned. "What we have done via this review is identified where, as agencies, we failed, admitted to those failings and begun working better together to help ensure every possible measure is put in place to try to prevent such a tragedy happening in the future," he told the room.

Laura Johnston, too, was apologetic. "We let Georgia down, we let Steve and Lynnette down, we let Jadine down. And as you'll see in the report, some of the young people referred to, we let them down as well. It's as simple as that," she said. "We should have been better at making sure that the risks to all the young people affected were considered."

But it had all come too late for our Georgia.

As Jadine said: "Why the hell did I not find out about this years ago? If I'd known, Georgia could have had a warning, and she'd still be with us today. They said they did everything possible to protect me from harm, but from where I'm sitting, nothing at all was done."

Then it was Steve's turn. We all had a copy of the MAPPA review, and Steve held his up. "We cried when we read this," he said. "And we cried even more when we read the Devon and Cornwall report, and the answers to why officers didn't do what they should have done. In our eyes it's ten times worse. It's an embarrassment to the police – and I think it should come out because it gives you the answers. The MAPPA is only half the story. It's like reading a novel, but closing it halfway through and not knowing the end."

Stood watching at the back of the room was Karen Manners. She must have been seething. David Shaw called out to her: "Have we got any plans to publish the Devon and Cornwall report?"

"I don't think so, not at the moment," she told him.

"I think we'd better have another think about that," Shaw said.

From there, we went from room to room, giving individual interviews. West Mercia had assigned a young girl from their press office to accompany us, and she dutifully followed us around taking notes. As Steve and I gave an interview to one reporter, we spotted the press liaison girl standing close by, listening and scribbling in her pad.

"Hang on," I said to her. "Are you writing down what we're saying?" I didn't want her pulling Steve up on it at work.

"I'm just making some notes about the questions," she stammered, completely flummoxed.

"This is our time to talk," I said.

"Yeah, we're not having that," Steve added. "This is a private conversation." With that, Steve took her pad off her, tore out a couple of pages, and handed it back.

I remember one TV interview, where Steve brandished his copy of Operation Columbia.

"These officers shouldn't sleep at night because they let Georgia down," he said.

I nodded. "They killed Georgia by not dealing with Reynolds properly – and they should face the consequences."

Consequences. That was the big question now – what consequences would these officers face? The rot had set in with their bungled investigation. Yes, plenty of mistakes had followed, but as far as we were concerned, the buck stopped with West Mercia. The betrayal hurt even more because until losing Georgia, I'd had nothing but praise for the police. I'd always stuck up for them, always believed officers gave the job nothing less than 100% – just like Steve and his MIU colleagues. But now I felt like I'd been kicked in the stomach.

About a month after the press conference, in November 2015, we were invited to sit in on the four officers' disciplinary hearings at the force HQ – Hindlip Hall in Worcestershire.

Alice was there, too, sat at the back with a Victim Support volunteer at her side. The poor girl looked absolutely broken. This, surely, was going to be our moment. Retribution. Everything had been building to it: the meetings, the questioning and digging, the tears and the anger we felt as each new failing was uncovered – all culminating in two damning reports. And now this hearing. Each officer would be questioned in turn by Superintendent Mark Travis, who would then decide what action to take.

As the hearing got underway, my heart began to sink. There was no sense at all that this was a serious matter, or that the officers were there to face appropriately serious consequences. They should have been quaking in their boots, but there was no trepidation.

I remember Dick selling Travis a big sob story about the pressures of being an inspector – and actually getting sympathy in return. Poor Dick with his overflowing in-tray. He still didn't think he'd done anything wrong. At one point, we were told he wanted to turn around and address us directly.

"No thank you," I said. Whatever Dick had to say, it was far too late in the day for me. I didn't even want to look at his face.

Steve took a different tack. "I'll hear him out, so long as I can say a few words in reply," he said. But that wasn't going to fly – he was turned down flat.

Only Jo Delahay got anything approaching a proper grilling. She came across as cocky and arrogant, and even she tried to garner sympathy, saying that she'd stuck it out at work even with the investigation and disciplinary hanging over her head. Hardly the mark of a hero.

The Youth Offending Team officer was a wet blanket. Fay Osmund-Smith seemed subdued and uncertain as she answered the superintendent's questions, taking her cue from the Police Federation representative sat beside her.

The hearings lasted all day, and as we waited in a side room for the panel's decision, I felt like it had all been a monstrous waste of effort.

"I've had harsher cross-examinations in court!" Steve said. "It's like a bunch of naughty school children getting a ticking off from the headmaster."

Alice had been reduced to tears. Everyone seemed to have forgotten that she'd been just a frightened, vulnerable 16-year-old when Jamie had strangled her, or that she could have easily lost her life in that struggle in his hallway. It was disgusting. "They don't believe me," she said. "I know how this is going to end. They're all going to go off and live their lives as if nothing's happened."

I despaired. Depressing as it was, I had to agree with Alice. The whole thing was a charade. They were going through the motions. I felt like I was being given a pat on the head. *There you go – there's your disciplinary. On your way now.*

In a way, the outcome had been decided long before we'd walked in that morning. Months back, during his tantrum at

Ferret Fest, Dick Langton had scoffed that we weren't going to get what we wanted – for officers to be sacked. I hate to say that he'd been right. Columbia had concluded that none of the officers' failures amounted to gross misconduct, so they were never going to lose their jobs. I don't think I'd realised at the time that we'd been watching what's called a 'misconduct meeting', and the most serious sanction any of them could face was a final written warning. So I gasped when the superintendent read out his decisions: Osmund-Smith and Dick would receive 'management advice' – the lowest outcome available – and Delahay would get a written warning. Slapped wrists all round. In the case of the Youth Offending Team officer, the superintendent found no evidence of misconduct.

At a later hearing, Evidence Review Manager Louise Hill was told that she, too, would receive a written warning. I despaired. It made no sense at all. Dick Langton had somehow even managed to land a promotion *while* he was under investigation.

It was over. We'd been fighting for justice for our Georgia for two-and-a-half years. Despite the shortcomings of their own officers, West Mercia Police said there was 'no causal link' between their failures and Georgia's death. The MAPPA, the Devon and Cornwall inquiry and now the disciplinaries all felt like they'd been a massive waste of time.

I was at a loss. I had no fight left in me. I couldn't think of any way forward.

I couldn't – but someone else could.

NINETEEN

Steve and I sat glued to the TV watching the BBC evening regional news bulletin.

"Here we go," I said, as the broadcast cut to their journalist standing in front of Wellington police station. She was reporting on the disciplinaries, and I'd handed her my copy of the Devon and Cornwall report – complete with the names of all the officers involved. One by one, she read them out, detailing the pitifully lenient outcomes they'd received in the farcical misconduct meeting we'd just sat through.

If it had been up to West Mercia Police, those names would never have seen the light of day – which had made me even more determined. It was a tiny, hard-won victory for us, and I punched the air. *Yes!* Their identities were now out in the open. They'd been named and shamed.

The force did, finally, publish Operation Columbia on their website – but even managed to mess that up. It might have been funny if it hadn't been so tragic and dangerous. They tried to protect their own officers by blacking out their names, but published the identities of two girls who'd either been attacked by Jamie or featured in his doctored photos. Both had been granted lifelong anonymity in the course of Jamie's conviction. The report was live on West Mercia's website for 11 days and was downloaded almost 200 times before someone spotted the error. By the skin of their teeth, West Mercia escaped prosecution for contempt of court. It was yet another embarrassing public humiliation for a force Steve had once been so proud to serve.

Now, any sense of pride had been smothered by resentment and bitterness. Steve – his anger simmering – was like a pressure cooker. His mental health was slipping into the abyss. In desperation, we booked a private appointment with a psychiatrist, who gave Steve a stark diagnosis: he was suffering from post traumatic stress disorder. The pain of losing Georgia, the strain of being a detective first and a grieving dad second, and the years he'd spent investigating the most horrific crimes had all taken their toll. It explained why, long after I'd gone to bed, Steve would sometimes find himself on our driveway about to tear off down the street to go and 'save' Georgia. Other traumas that he'd suppressed and buried deep were breaking through to the surface, not least having to identify the photos of Georgia's last moments – and what came after. I didn't know how long Steve could hang on. Once again, our own futures looked uncertain.

But the Police Federation had an idea. After having Jamie Reynolds' 'human rights' rammed down our throats for years, they suggested suing West Mercia Police using the exact same piece of legislation. They thought they could argue that by failing to protect Georgia, the force had breached Article 2 of the European Convention on Human Rights – the right to life – as well as Article 3, the right to protection from degrading and inhuman treatment.

We met with a Federation lawyer in Birmingham to talk it through.

"What do you want out of this?" he asked us.

We did need some kind of safety blanket in place in case Steve crumbled, but any financial consideration was secondary. The main thing we wanted was for West Mercia to hold their hands up, rather than waving around their 'no causal link' line like it was a get out of jail free card. I won't lie – I wanted to hurt them. I wanted to make them squirm.

"I'd like them to admit they've done something wrong," I said.

The feedback from the Federation barrister was encouraging. Their view was – of course there was a causal link. The police have a duty to protect the public. Georgia was a member of the public, and West Mercia had had plenty of warning that Jamie Reynolds was targeting young women. But prising an admission out of them wouldn't be easy. It was practically unheard of.

Over the next few months, our claim was batted back and forth between West Mercia's lawyers and ours, organised by the Police Federation. Then in May 2016 we were invited to London to thrash out a settlement. Scarlett joined us, too, and we sat around a conference table with solicitors and barristers from both sides. The day was a blur, but I remember long periods where we were left alone with our thoughts in this huge room while the suits negotiated in private. They'd return and lay out an offer – and we'd send them away again. It took me back to the time three years previously when we'd sat in our bedroom bay window, looking out for Georgia – the sense that we were not part of the world, that we were just watching from a distance. Or that we were in the eye of a tornado, observing a maelstrom swirling around us. It wasn't real. It wasn't happening. Our lives hadn't really come to this.

At one point, our barrister asked Steve if there was anything he wanted to say. In case they'd forgotten just why we were all there, Steve began laying out what had happened to our daughter, describing how Jamie had killed her, and detailing our loss.

"These officers let a murderer go," Steve said, jabbing the table.

The barrister intervened, shutting him down. "OK. Thank you, Steve. That's enough."

The whole process felt cold and calculated. I remember another moment when the lawyers returned and told us they could offer the equivalent of a couple of thousand euros. Until then, I'd managed to keep a lid on my emotions but, at that, the seal was broken and they came flooding out.

"It's disgusting that you think our daughter's life is worth so little!" I railed, tears streaming. How was a bit of pocket change going to hurt West Mercia? "You're laughing at us! And what if Steve loses his job? How do we survive then? How do we pay for the therapists and counsellors he needs? We're not rich people! I can't stand this!"

As my rant gave way to sobs, Scarlett caught on my coat tails. "That's my little sister! She should still be alive. We shouldn't be here, we shouldn't have to fight all the time!"

We'd bared our souls to them. We'd made it real. Stunned into silence, the suits shuffled out to think again. Each time they returned, their offer improved. The wording of West Mercia's admission of failure grew more distinct as we chipped away at its meaning.

The Federation lawyer was eager for us to settle. If the case went to court, he said, it could take years. The Federation would only cover the legal costs to a certain point – and then it would be down to us. We could lose our home. Everything.

It was late in the evening and everyone else in the barristers' chambers had gone home for the day when the lawyers finally came back with something we were half-way happy with. I say halfway because really, we felt backed into a corner. With hindsight, we should have hunkered down and dug our heels in. But we were exhausted, we'd reached the end of the road.

West Mercia Police admitted – in writing – that they breached their obligation to protect Georgia's life under Articles 2 and 3 of the Human Rights Act. We agreed a sum of money to safeguard our own futures, a treatment fund for Steve and a settlement for Scarlett. On top of that, the force agreed to pay a sum to The Georgia Williams Trust – and I knew exactly what I was going to do with it.

Steve clung on for another three years in the police, but the writing was on the wall long before he took early retirement. He couldn't abide laziness and incompetence – and saw plenty. At times he'd over-react and blow up in a rage. His stress levels were off the scale. One day, seeing his GP, he collapsed in the surgery. The warning was dire: working as a detective was shortening his lifespan. It was a tragic waste – Steve still had plenty to give and had always intended to work for as long as he was fit. If he'd had the choice, he'd have stayed until well into his 70s. But for the sake of his sanity and his health, he had to step away. In 2019, he took early retirement. Years on, the aftershock of Jamie Reynolds' despicable crime was still wreaking havoc. To this day, Steve is still undergoing trauma therapy.

Those training sessions that West Mercia had been so keen to involve us in? They never really materialised. We were invited to one, along with Jadine, organised by Telford and Wrekin Council and attended by social workers and police officers. They told us afterwards it wouldn't have had half the impact if we hadn't taken part. After years of fight and negativity, I felt as though we were doing something positive. But that was it – we were never invited again.

And yet what happened to Georgia is as relevant today as ever. I read news stories of women losing their lives at the hands of men, of corrupt, inept, sexually abusive and even murderous police officers. I hear the same, tired lines trotted out time and time again – not least in the Telford grooming scandal, another shameful episode in West Mercia's history. *We got it wrong. We let people down. Our public deserves better. Lessons have been learned.* But nothing really changes.

Through Georgia's Trust, and off my own back, I go into schools and talk to the kids about what happened to Georgia. Sometimes it overwhelms me, but I feel that if I can make a difference – if I can spare one family from the pain we've suffered – I have to do it, for Georgia's sake.

I tell them to trust their instincts, that if something doesn't feel right, it generally isn't. I tell them that if they feel off about someone, they must reach out for help. I talk to them about pornography, often triggering embarrassed sniggers and laughter from the boys.

"You might think it's funny, and that's fine – but it can lead you down a very dark road," I tell them. "Unfortunately for us and for Georgia, that's where Jamie Reynolds got to. And now he's locked up, forever, because he took her life."

With the older college students, I might talk to them about snuff movies. Often, kids think these horrors exist only online – warped fantasies flickering on their laptop screens and phones. But then I see their faces blanch, the shock sinking in, as the realisation hits home: sometimes these digital horrors punch through into reality. Sometimes they wash up on your doorstep.

And I talk about The Georgia Williams Trust. Ten years on, it's still going strong. It's one way of keeping Georgia's memory alive. We give grants to schools and individual children. We set up a groundbreaking scuba-diving scholarship, send kids on volunteer missions overseas, sponsor sports day trophies and fund gym equipment and musical instruments. I know that for some kids, the help has literally been life changing. Georgia always dreamt big, and I like to think that in some way we're helping make dreams come true.

I said I knew exactly how we'd spend the compensation money secured by the Trust from West Mercia Police. By this time, Georgia's old school had finished building the plane she'd started work on all those years ago, and I couldn't imagine a more fitting tribute to her than buying it from Boeing, to give disabled and disadvantaged kids a taste of flying.

One grey and dreary day, we drove down to Halfpenny Green airport near Wolverhampton for the official handover. The plane had been registered with the initials GWFT – standing for 'Georgia Williams Ferret'. I remember someone pointing out a bit of the cockpit that Georgia had been working on, and having to choke back a sob. "I hope she did those screws up nice and tight," I joked, trying to make light of it. Inside, I felt like I was being torn apart.

"Do you want to go for a flight?" someone asked.

"Me?" I said, uncertain. "Erm… OK!"

I squeezed in beside the pilot and he helped strap me in. As we sat on the runway waiting to take off, I thought – inevitably – of Georgia. It should have been her in the cockpit, her mates waving her off, as they all enjoyed the fruits of their labour. She'd wanted to be one of the first to fly in the plane, so it felt wrong somehow to be taking her place, realising a dream she'd held so dearly. *She'd have absolutely bloody loved this,* I thought. *She'd probably have been a pilot by now.* I was sure she was laughing her socks off at me, so far out of my comfort zone.

Just before we set off taxiing down the runway, the clouds parted to reveal blue skies, and the previously dull day was now drenched in sunshine. Then we were heading off, the whine of the plane's engine reaching fever pitch. I left my tummy behind as we lifted off the tarmac, and we climbed high into the sky. Looking out of the window, I gazed at the patchwork quilt fields below.

LYNNETTE WILLIAMS

All of a sudden, a huge bird of prey soared up in front of us. The pilot and I gasped, and he let go a nervous chuckle. "You know – that hardly ever happens," he laughed. "I bet Georgia has done that to give you a scare!"

My chest hitched, but I smiled and nodded. "Yes," I said. "I think she probably has."

THE END

ACKNOWLEDGEMENTS

Thanks first of all to Paul Hopwood for being a great friend, through thick and thin. Also to Tony Skelding who helped by taking the stresses off us with all the funeral arrangements, not to mention supplying us with biscuits! Thank you to Aide McGee for fighting our corner, and to Frank Malloy for your advice and guidance when we thought we'd hit a brick wall. To the M.I.U. team at Telford – thank you all for securing the justice Georgia deserved, ensuring peace of mind for our family. And to the people of Telford – thank you for all your support. To the trustees of the Georgia Williams Trust past and present – you've put your hearts into helping others. Thank you! To Mardle Books, we're so grateful to you for making it possible to get the true story told. And lastly but not least – dear Robin, thank you for your understanding and patience. I know I've not made it easy going, reliving events has been hard, but your care has made it possible.